Rev. Ken's Little Book on Marriage & Weddings

Rev. Ken's Little Book on Marriage & Weddings

Ken JP Stuczynski

AmorphousPublishingGuild

Amorphous Publishing Guild

Buffalo, NY USA

www.Amorphous.Press

To all the couples
I've helped wed,
May they find the best in life
and each other

Contents

Introduction

To talk about weddings, we should talk about marriage. Cultures that place a high value on the ceremony are said to have more lasting marriages. But there are those who have fantasized about the perfect wedding so long, the choice of spouse seems irrelevant. One can only hope they put as much effort into what happens after the Big Day.

Whatever the wedding, big or small, extravagant or humble, it should be meaningful. I've been to expensive weddings that didn't seem as joyous as one would expect. I've also had a bride tell me she got the wedding of their dreams — in the backyard of their apartment with plasticware and plastic chairs. I've seen tears of joy in the unlikeliest of places. We can worry too much about the perfect day to remember, or fear it won't be good enough.

We can plan for every contingency. We can, and probably should, leave as little to chance as possible. But something unexpected will always happen, and it is that you will remember. But something "going wrong" is about perspective. It may be that special something in the telling of your story. It may not have been desired at the time, but it will bring a smile to your face as long as you live.

Instead of a fantasy acted out in mere costumes, that day can be a snapshot of where a couple is in their life at that moment, a real part of their story. It's not separate from the story. In other words, a wedding can be an amazing moment in a relationship, but it's not the relationship. It's not the marriage. I believe that by the time you tie the knot, you are already married in spirit. The wedding is just the outward manifestation. It's sharing what is already there with your loved ones and the world. It's "making it official".

That's why the first part of this book is about the marriage, not the ceremony. If you skip forward out of excitement, that's okay. But if you don't care about the rest, ask yourself why. Maybe you're confident you don't need any "pre-marriage counselling". But there's a reason I offer it to all my couples. There's a reason they are grateful for my "Pre-Cana" discussion (explained in that chapter). It's not really counselling, and certainly not preaching — it's advice many wish they had been told when they got married.

It's also a chance to get to know the couple. I makes it possible to custom-tailor a ceremony and rituals that reflect the couple's unique life journey. It enables me to craft something that reflects and honors their sometimes diverse faith traditions. Many officiants just show up for the day, and the couple gets what they get. I'd rather be and give more than that. Why not go over things that need to be done, and make them aware of countless details and options they may not have thought of? That is what this book is about — for their wedding and their life together.

A Note About Language

Throughout this book, I focus on the conventional roles of the Bride and Groom in the context of modern weddings in the United States and similar cultures. None of this is meant to imply that these traditions or expectations are better or worse than other traditions and choices.

Most suggestions will work regardless of being a same-sex couple, while other suggestions may not make sense in that context.

I also use the term *Maid of Honor* as it would equally apply to a *Matron of Honor*. I speak of a *Best Man*, but maybe you choose two people for that role. Examples of variations are limitless.

It would be too exhausting to write these caveats into every chapter. In other words, forgive my limitations of language and space. I wrote this book for everyone, without judgment. It can be as useful as you see fit to use it!

Pre-Cana

My wife and I chose to get married within our family tradition, Roman Catholicism. One of the requirements was to go to classes called "Pre-Cana", a reference to the story in the Gospels about the wedding where Jesus turned water into wine. But it wasn't about the story, and it wasn't religious education, per se. It was more about deeply considering why you are getting married and what to expect.

There were many speakers on many topics. An elderly couple, married most of their lives to each other, gave their advice. A nurse talked about sex. But, oddly enough, it was the celibate priest, who counselled couples for many years, who seemed to give the most useful advice.

With my own diverse personal and educational background, I felt it would be best that I offer something similar. I have a couple of worksheets that couples said are helpful (see "My Spouse's Instruction Manual" and "Values Clarification Worksheet" in the back of this book).

But most of what I cover is showing where the landmines are. I have found life is much easier when you are aware of the things that can ruin it and then not do those things.

Even little things can become big things. Or you have unrealistic expectations and then get angry that they cannot be met. Sometimes people change the moment they get married, but more often, it's the hope they will change once they are married that is the problem. A wedding isn't meant to solve a problem, shotguns aside.

A survey was done of divorced couples, asking them two simple questions: what about the other person made you want to marry them; and what about them made you want a divorce. The surprising result was that the reasons for marrying and divorcing were the same things! Of course, they were worded differently. She married him because she was shy and needed someone outgoing to bring her out of her shell. She divorced him because he's out too much with the guys. He married her because she was a party girl. He divorced her because she was an addict.

Or sometimes the connection is based too much on commonality. A couple may get married because they were on a mountain-climbing team and got divorced when injuries and arthritis kicked in, finding they had little else in common.

And then there's time. People change. It's not just that sex is questionable in a nursing home and things like wrinkles happen. We grow, as we should. But can we grow together? That is why you must know your partner well enough to see their core personality — those things that make them who they are, regardless of fortune, health, and age. If you fall in love with that, you may never really "fall out of love".

If you "fell in love" in the sense of a powerful connection here and now, that is usually not enough. Longstanding love isn't so much yearning and burning as commitment and cooperation built on trust, respect, and providing a safe space for each other. Soulmates can make it work, for better or for worse. Best friends can make it work. Fiery, passionate, and intense relationships are not sustainable and can even be destructive. Or they can be a start if you're lucky enough to have it blossom into something more. Your body may tell you this or that person is attractive. Your brain may tell you that you want to have a family with them. And your heart may tell you you want to spend eternity with them. But most people are conflicted because few people, if anyone, fall into all three categories.

But let's assume you have confidence that you're joining for all the right reasons. What is on the road ahead? What are your odds? At some point, I ask couples if they are living together. This isn't to judge them but to reassure them that statistically, it seems to make little difference in rates of divorce. What about meeting online? Nearly half of all American marriages today start with couples who met online, and the rate of reported satisfaction is surprisingly *higher* than in other marriages.

Keep in mind, these are just statistics. We're not talking causation, and one couple is a personal reality, not a statistic. But there are so many things you can do to have a successful marriage, not just a great wedding. So let's get started on exploring the road ahead.

Do Opposites Attract?

Yes, opposites attract. And sometimes, opposites attract trouble. It's good to have different strengths and weaknesses. It's good to need and depend on each other for some things. And you should share some basic values, even if you may have very different personalities and interests.

Spending time apart isn't a bad thing. My wife's mother joked that the secret to a successful marriage is working different shifts. Sometimes, being home all the time after retirement or some other circumstance can drive the other person nuts! It's okay to need some personal space. Some couples sleep better in separate beds, which was the norm for a long time in many families. The trick is to be aware, accept it, and not take it personally.

My wife and I, on the other hand, *never* get tired of each other. When I was starting a new business at home and she was between jobs, we saw each other 24 hours a day. What did I do when I needed to get out of the house? I took her with me! But that is not normal, or to be expected in most relationships.

Your spouse shouldn't be expected to be all things to you either. Sometimes you need someone to blow off steam with while the other isn't available or it's just not a good time. Maybe you need to talk about or do things your spouse isn't interested in. In fact, you *need* to have experiences outside the relationship to have something to bring back into it.

There's also doing different roles at different times. According to one model, there are three roles in a situation you can play: the Parent; the Adult; and the Child. We all need to be babied sometimes. We all have an instinct to care for or pamper a loved one. And sometimes we want to be carefree. You can figure out which is which. The point is that you can play with these roles. Sometimes you both have to be the adult and it's annoying when one plays the child. Or we feel too grown up to have fun when the other one wants to just let their hair down or be silly. Sometimes the child in us needs some reigning in. And sometimes both must play the role of adult and deal with things.

Knowing this dynamic can give you permission to really embrace different roles in different situations. It will take away the need for judgment and can strengthen bonds of friendship, intimacy, interdependence, and commitment.

Hunters and Gatherers

They say men are from Mars and women are from Venus. Geography aside, people are not all wired the same. Men tend to have certain psychological traits and women others. Men tend to be better at math then language, and women are the flip side of that. But these are just statistics. All bets are off for real people.

Some things are cultural, but there really does seem to be some genetic reality to it. In distant times past, men were hunters and women were gatherers. It's a painful oversimplification if you're an anthropologist, but there's real truth to it, even today. Let me prove it.

When I meet with a couple, the man is usually a hunter and the woman a gatherer. Sometimes it's reversed. In same-sex couples, there also tends to be complementary yet different roles and traits. One person is too hot when they sleep and the other is too cold, for example. I joke that if you can agree on room temperature, you probably shouldn't be married.

Almost always, one of them prefers a map, and the other one uses landmarks to find their way. Here's where it gets interesting. Tell the one who is comfortable with a map that they need to look at every object in the fridge to find what they are looking for. Then tell the one who uses landmarks that they can just reach in and grab what they want. It's like being psychic. But it's really that one is a hunter (the map, picking out items) and the other a gatherer (landmarks, just seeing what they need).

It can be frustrating that a hunter doesn't want to ask for directions. And it's frustrating that a gatherer doesn't know what you mean when you say go "North" instead of "left". But you can accept it and joke about it.

The same is true for another very important aspect of life — problem-solving.

Generally speaking, men want to solve problems; women want to feel supported in addressing issues. Regardless of who is what, this dynamic causes friction. One gets frustrated because offering a solution doesn't seem to help, and the other feels like their emotional needs are being ignored. If you are one or the other, you can't help it. Neither can they. It takes an acceptance of that to not turn it into a longstanding problem.

This is really about the virtue of listening, and it works both ways. Jumping up to get to work on a problem isn't listening. Giving advice isn't listening. Sympathizing, encouraging, or sharing your own feelings is good, but it's not listening. Listen first. If you're eager to help, it requires all the more patience. The silence can be deafening. Brave through it. Embrace it! Just holding each other or sitting in silence can be profound and healing.

Be aware of the other person's feelings and how their mind works. At least try to tune into their frequency and forgive when they have trouble tuning into yours. (See "Your Spouse's Instruction Manual" at the back of this book.) This tolerance and effort apply to every difference in personalities, much of which will never magically change, before or after marriage.

Love Languages

We all express our affections in certain ways more than others. Usually, it's what we are used to based on the household we grew up in. Some families show physical affection, and some not so much. Some say "I love you" and others do not. Gift-giving may be the norm. Maybe it's more about the amount of time spent together, or picking up slack around the house in terms of chores. Sometimes, it's just a personality trait as to how a person prefers expressions of love.

They really are like languages. Some of us are bilingual, so to speak. We can appreciate more than one way to express how much we care. But we are usually deaf to some of them.

Words themselves mean different things in different love languages. If you were brought up to think words and promises were superficial, you may never say "I love you". Your partner, who grew up hearing it all their childhood, may feel so offended they demand, "Why don't you ever say it?" The response is also hurt feelings, something like "How can you think I don't love you? Do I have to say it?"

Some people feel loved when they receive tokens of affection. Flowers, chocolate, jewelry, or cufflinks may all brighten one person's day. To another, they may actually feel bribed, or like the other person is trying too hard to prove something.

Or maybe it's problematic due to trauma. If someone was physically abused, they may not be comfortable with intimacy or even touch. That can be a challenge for a partner who craves such contact. They may be self-conscious and have a negative body image. You may find them the most beautiful person in the world, but a compliment will still not feel sincere to them.

The point is for each to learn the other person's languages, and which ones they are not comfortable with. It's hard to respect boundaries when you want to share every part of your soul with them, but that is part of who they are.

Approach this from three directions. Try to speak languages they understand; try to acknowledge their expressions of love; and forgive them when they just can't do these things themselves.

Awareness is key. If you know what the dynamic is, you may still feel hurt or hurtful. But you will be much better at not judging them or yourself. Not being physically affectionate isn't the same as being a "cold" human being. Not saying "I love you" doesn't mean they don't. And not being able to do some of these isn't always a matter of choice or willpower. And none of this needs to drive a wedge that grows over time. Pull the wedge out now. Awareness can become acceptance.

Arguing

If you never argue, you probably don't communicate. However, advice I heard long ago was that it is a bad sign if you argue regularly — except in the last several weeks before a wedding! Stressful times cause stressful reactions, and we tend to take it out on those closest to us. Why? Maybe because they are there, or maybe because we know we'll be tolerated and forgiven. That's not terrible, so long as you don't make them feel you are taking them for granted.

Everyone has a right to disagree. And everyone has a right to be upset. There will be misunderstandings no matter how much you finish each other's sentences.

Sometimes it's like my wife and I share the same brain — we can hold a conversation with looks and nods, and even sigh at the same time. Other times, it's like we are different species, particularly with directions and instructions. Then there are bad habits or behaviors that we can't let go of, even though they annoy the other person. I'm a terror with potty humor ... but I'll spare the reader and save that for another book.

But how do you make the best of it? First, fight fair. Be very careful about showing disrespect to something dear to the other person. Don't EVER criticize how a mother keeps their house. Don't EVER criticize a father's ability to provide. In most cultures, these are sacred spaces, and attacking them is hitting below the belt. That doesn't mean pretending the other person is perfect in those respects, but it does mean they are likely to be deeply sensitive about criticism. Offer to help, and be aware they may not want you to. Don't push the issue.

Events in the past may be important, but don't bring them up as ammunition in an argument. If you forgive them, let it go, even if you cannot forget. This isn't about burying feelings. This is about not lashing out in ways that hurt just to hurt them. This may go without saying, but we're only human and tempers can flare. The goal is not to say anything you can't take back.

Money is the number one topic of disharmony, especially in tough times. One or both partners may be bad at managing it. It may just be a constant frustration and worry. And a partner who has it ingrained in them to be the provider doesn't take well any perceived inability to do so. There is a particularly high rate of divorce among couples where the woman makes more money than the man. It doesn't have to be this way. It's often an uncontrollable, subconscious pressure. Being aware of it and expressing it releases that pressure.

Here's a life hack: hold hands when you argue. Sitting down and doing this makes it very difficult for tensions to flare out of control. It may turn to tears, and that's okay.

A less obvious life hack: texting. If you just can't talk about something calmly, go to different rooms and text each other.

Give each other time to type (and repeatedly delete and retype) a more careful message. And sometimes you can say things is a "digital letter" that you can't say face-to-face.

Find what works for you. Sometimes one approach will work better than another, depending on the situation. And realize what your partner can't say. As much as you may need them to, they just can't. If you just can't talk about or do something, express that and ask them to accept it.

Feelings are strange things. We can't help having them. They are NOT truths or need to define our actions. Sometimes, how we feel offends the ones we love. Ask for forgiveness, even though this is not about fault. They need to know you can't just turn them off or hide them. And you need to give them the same courtesy.

Like everything else we've talked about, awareness is key. If you realize what is going on, you can step back a little, breathe, regroup, and resolve or let go.

On a side note, pretending or repressing dissatisfaction is not good in the long run. It will still affect your feelings and judgment. And if you hide it even from yourself, you may blow up at some point. It will be an utter surprise to you. But it didn't come from nowhere. That's the time to sit down and try and process your feelings. Include your spouse whenever you are able, especially if you lost it while they were in the blast radius.

Often it's friendly jabs. You consciously know it's in jest. It's not mean-spirited. But your subconscious doesn't know that. Maybe you are more self-conscious about something than you thought. If you release the "charge" of whatever it is, you can go on as before, perhaps a bit more careful not to overdo joking criticisms.

Children

Some people say the purpose of marriage is to have children. Then again, for most of history, marriage was basically ownership of women and a paper trail for inheritance. In some cultures and families, you're practically expected to provide grandchildren. But it must be your choice, as a couple.

If you want to have children, have them. Foster them. Adopt them. Or don't. But at least talk about them. And don't assume you will never have to have the conversation — thought that is far less likely with same-sex couples!

Willingness to have or not have children is a deal-breaker for most people. It's even grounds for divorce or annulment in many places. Marriage doesn't have to be to start a family, but that is a sort of default setting in society. Maybe not for you, but be clear about that before you "trap" each other out of major life goals they may (or may not) have.

How you raise children can be complicated. There needs to be agreement or compromise on all those things you may wish for or expect in your life together. We'll cover some aspects of that in the chapters ahead.

Family Cultures

As an Interfaith minister, I specialize in working with couples and families of different religious backgrounds. Sometimes, there are incompatibilities of customs, religious or otherwise. But the truth is that EVERY couple is mixed to some extent. Even if they come from households that have a similar religious background and ethnicity, each family has its own distinct *familial* culture.

Perhaps the most important consideration is beliefs about roles, especially on the question of parenting. Will there be a distinct "Man of the house", or will the family be more matriarchal? How our own parents related to each other and their children – for better or worse – becomes the subconscious default template. We need to be aware of how much that can influence our feelings, and if unexamined, our behaviors. The truth is that we don't have to follow it. We may not *want* to follow it, or it may be important to us, and our partner must be accepting of that.

We tend to be attracted to partners who share some personality traits with one of our parents. Sometimes, that sets up an unreasonable expectation. When my wife needs something built,

I have to remind her that I'm not her dad, who simply went to the basement and in a few moments — PRESTO! Mind you, I can build a nice shelf when I need to. Heck, I remodeled our dining room into a library and can fix or install various things. But she came from a family where her mother said she wanted a window raised because her fiberglass curtains were too long — and he did exactly that. I am thankfully forgiven that I am not willing or able to do that. It's a point of amusement at times.

Sometimes, it's not so easy. Sometimes it's about trauma. We may expect our partner to act like our parent acted. It could be a fear of abandonment, alcoholism, or even violence. You might flinch if they raise their voice or get angry, even if they would never hurt you. Consciously, you know they are not that person, but your subconscious sneaks in and whispers otherwise. Trauma, even with a small "t", is hardwired in our brains. It's not something you can control. Counselling may be helpful or even necessary, and there is no shame in that. But it could seriously harm your relationship if ignored.

Even if there is some basic incompatibility, that doesn't mean it can't work. My stepmother made it clear once that "The Man is the head of the household, and he has final say in all things", while my father meekly replied, "Yes, dear". Other times, it's a challenge. For example, I am more maternal in my parental instincts, and that made my daughter's mother feel like I was encroaching on her role as mother. Sometimes you just deal with it until the circumstances pass.

No matter what it is, talk it through. If possible, do so before you have to deal with it, or small things become big things. Turn potential conflict over differences into planning a composite way of life you can both appreciate.

Religion

When I meet with couples, I always ask how their children may be raised in terms of religion. This can come off as preachy, but that is never my intention. It is an opportunity to share advice.

We all have what I call a "relationship with life". Other people call it *religion*. In it's most basic sense, it's the way we, individually and collectively, choose to experience life and what we believe about existence. It usually involves rituals or willful habits, and may or may not have anything to do with formal religion. It may not have anything to do with a belief in a Supreme Being. But each person has some relationship with life that is expressed in their values and actions.

So what does this have to do with marriage? You may celebrate different holidays. One of you may make a big deal out of birthdays and the other doesn't. You may want your children to grow up in the sacraments or rites of a particular faith tradition. It might mean a Baptism or Christening when they are born, or religious education classes. Will there be a Bar Mitzvah or Quinceañera? These are all things to discuss.

But my advice is, PLEASE don't raise them without either parent's traditions, waiting for them to decide when they are older. If parents spoke two different languages, would it make sense not to teach them either until they are "old enough to decide"? This doesn't mean cramming dogma down their throats. However, they should have *some* spiritual language they can explore, and then accept or reject when they are older. But without a frame of reference to begin with, how can they even consider such things? And even the subtlest traditions may become deeply meaningful to them when they have children.

It could be a simple grace at meals, or covering the mirrors in the house after the death of a loved one. It could be a little altar with a candle and statues, or prayer cards tucked on a windowsill. It could be setting a day apart for rest. It could be crossing yourself before you go onto the sports field. It could be chalk on a doorpost or the smell of incense. It could be something you yourself grew up with, or a new tradition you start as a family. It could be music and songs with special words.

Sometimes, having children helps us reconnect with our own roots. Why cut down the tree? Make new branches for your descendants to hang their own traditions on someday.

Falling in Love (Again)

In modern times, people tend to live longer lives. So long, in fact, that they can have and raise a family, then do it all over again. Maybe that's where mid-life crisis comes from. Living much past child-rearing years leaves room for ... well, that's the question. Some studies have shown that the happiest time in a couple's lives is after their children go off on their own. Other people experience "Empty Nest Syndrome". But the point of this chapter is to talk about the fact that we may fall in love more than once over the years.

The problem is that it may not be with your spouse every time. Buckle up, because if you're willing to hear what I'm saying, it will all be alright.

Like birds impress on their parent (or anyone perching near them at the right time), we can get fixated on someone. There are usually emotional and sexual components to this. That's "falling in love". The less romantic term is INFATUATION. Or call it a crush. The painful thing is when it's unrequited instead of mutual. It's even worse when someone solicits your love un-wholeheartedly, but you end up "head over heels". These games are for high school, but happen in adulthood.

It often starts with someone paying attention to you in your workplace. They know you're married but don't care, or convince themselves they would be better for you. They may encourage you to find fault in your marriage, even if there isn't any, or at least anything major. Maybe the attention flatters you, and you don't feel as valued at home in the hustle and bustle of raising a family. The primitive part of your brain kicks in, and you justify accepting the attention by fabricating an attitude of dissatisfaction in your marriage. You may not be doing this consciously. That's why you have to *look for it*. See the pattern. Don't follow the pattern.

But let's say you fall madly in love with someone who is not your spouse. I can't say this loudly enough: SO WHAT? Yes, it may be emotionally intense, at least for you. But did you get married *only* because you were "in love"? If you fall out of love, then what? Do you simply divorce and get married again to someone else you fall in love with? Do you then rinse, lather, and repeat? On the other hand, if you truly *choose* to be with someone, and accept growing together over years of life changes and circumstances — now that's a marriage. Recognize the other thing for what it is. Infatuation can be very powerful, but really, it's just ... annoying.

It really can be innocent or harmless. It's no secret that I always had a bit of a crush on a young woman whom I love and highly respect to this day. She is an amazing human being, and due to various circumstances, I also feel fatherly towards her. I just really want them as part of my family in some way. The hardest part was seeing her in bad relationships, knowing she deserved better. This wasn't some insincere rationalization for my own attraction. I know our friendship was the real connection because when she got married to a wonderful man, I found myself truly elated for her.

I also experienced an infatuation with someone during my mid-life crisis. But I was able to talk about it with my wife, and she was amazingly compassionate and patient about it. Because I recognized it for what it was, there was no way I was going to disrespect my commitments and potentially lose a true soulmate over such a thing. That was made clear to all involved. That level of openness and honesty may not be possible in some realationships, but aim for it. It's hard to unintentionally undermine someone's trust when you don't keep secrets from them.

It also doesn't help the chances of infidelity when I brag about my wife all the time ... gratitude keeps a multitude of sins at bay.

Values and Trust

We need to borrow a time machine for a moment. How do we picture ourselves a few decades from now, or at some late stage of life? Surely the same things won't be as important as they are today. Money and health may be more important, while travel and luxury may be more important now. Maybe social life is a priority now, but children and religion will be later.

Are you and your spouse on the same page regarding the future as well as goals for the next few years? Picture how you will see each other when you're no longer young. Looking forward to a "dad bod" or getting past menopause? Let's just say most people have mixed feelings. But it's a sign of true love when people look forward to growing old together.

There's another reason to go over various things that are more or less important to each other. Sometimes you may be fine with your spouse handling some matters, or even hope they will. Other times not so much. Maybe they are bad with money or family scheduling. Being comfortable with your spouse in terms of things like childcare or major purchases is important, but sometimes it's unrealistic. Sometimes they know and accept that.

But if you don't talk about it now, it may be harder later. Imagine finding out their dream is to live in the country and you're a city slicker to the core. What about medical proxy issues? How do you balance spending time with both of your families for holidays? Almost anything can become a problem. Almost anything can be worked out.

But unexpected aspects of your relationship can cause resentment. Work it out now, and forever hold your peace, so to speak.

(To address both values and trust, see the "Values Clarification Worksheet" at the back of this book.)

Veto Power

I do not believe a relationship should be 50/50. It's not a nego-
tiation. It's not a perfect balance to be achieved with guilt or
remorse when you don't.

It's more like 100/100. Each person does all they can, when
they can. But it's never meant to be "equal". There are times you
can't give 100% or even 50% and the other person tries to pick
up the slack. It could be illness, job issues, or just having a bad
day. One may be able to do more physically, financially, or emotionally. If you both had all the same abilities, you wouldn't need
both of you!

This is cause for some serious discussion. Who do you trust
more with balancing the checkbook? My wife has a darn hard
time doing it, but I stay out of that. Sometimes, having two people in the kitchen (metaphorically or physically) makes things
harder than working alone.

Speaking of kitchens, my wife and I truly live up to memes
that deal with the man always standing wherever the woman
needs to get to. It's frustrating, but comical. (The comical part is
optional, but necessary for a healthy relationship.) When we do

cook together, I'm her sous chef. Now and then the roles are re-versed. It's good to have one person in charge and the other help-ing. It never has to be the same person.

Here's the problem. You should never boss each other around, but sometimes one person must put their foot down. My wife and I even joke about it. If you REALLY need to get a pizza and the other person doesn't feel like it, let them have their way. Just use this superpower sparingly.

For more difficult matters, it comes down to trust. Sometimes a person is unable to see what is happening. Mental illness. Ad-diction. Obsession. Fanaticism. Being in a cult. In cases where in-tervention is necessary, the one afflicted needs to let their spouse invoke veto power, even if they can't accept the reality of it. Hav-ing a third-party can be especially helpful, just to make clear it isn't imagination, exaggeration, or gaslighting.

Such things can ruin not just a person's life, but that of those around them. There is no hope if there is no trust. You must al-low the issue to be addressed.

Planning

First an important note about planning the Big Day together. Both parties won't have the same interest in details. They may have certain wishes or general ideas. But it can be tough to navigate, particualry for the groom.

In modern American culture, it's still a very bride-focused event with the Bride's family generally organizing and even paying for quite a bit of it. The Groom often just nods their head or may give *too much* input. Sometimes it's a tightrope act to not appear disinterested while also not getting in the way. That isn't always an issue, but can either be frustrating or something to laugh about. Like most things in life, it's a choice.

As for the checklist, many of the chapters that follow hit key points. But there are basic things like deciding when and where to have your wedding. Booking certain dates on short notice or for holidays may be difficult. But you must also consider the elephant in the room, or rather, how many elephants – I mean guests – are you inviting?

You want both sides of the family (and friends) to be represented. Avoid blacklisting anyone unilaterally. Consider travel distances and be clear about expenses if it's a "destination" wedding. And there's nothing wrong with inviting people you know can't be there. They may pleasantly surprise you, or at least be grateful you thought of them. You could even send them favors afterward.

Before I meet with a couple, I have them fill out an online form to get things started. Apart from names and contact information, I ask for the date, time, and location of the event. I also ask about ceremony details and extras such as

- Reception location
- If a Blessing over the meal (grace) is requested
- Music for ceremony (live / portable / sound system & DJ)
- How many people are standing up (besides the couple)
- Who is presenting the bride, if any (walking down the aisle)
- Children or pets in the party (ring bearer / flower girl)
- Vows (traditional or self-written)

They may not have decided some of the details, but it makes the couple start thinking about them. I'm not trying to be a wedding planner, but most people don't have one, and the minister is in a unique position to make sure they don't miss major details. You certainly don't want things being dealt with last minute the day of the wedding — that can affect everyone's roles. As an officiant, I want them to know I'm on their team. And that is why I go into a lot more detail when we meet.

Most of these details and advice are found in the following chapters. Below are two particular things officiants and couples should discuss.

Religiosity

As an Interfaith minister, I found myself uniquely suited to weddings. So many people are unchurched or do not wish to have their ceremony at their own church for various reasons. Catholics in particular (the tradition of my own family growing up) sometimes have a difficult time meeting certain requirements, usually due to it being a second marriage. But most common are couples who are not religious but still want a spiritual service, acknowledging a higher being. They may be of different faith traditions and want elements of both. Or they may want something uniquely their own.

When I meet with a couple, I try to find out the "religiosity" of what they are looking for. It can be as religious or secular as they wish, so long as they don't ask for sacraments I'm not entitled to give. I also try to take into consideration their families and guests.

The feedback from my first wedding was that everyone experienced the service in their own spiritual language. Christians thought it was a beautiful Christian wedding; Pagans thought it was a beautiful Pagan service. It was my intention to use language that spoke to all those present, and I clearly found my talent and calling in that.

If you are not getting married in a ceremony of a particular religious tradition, communicate that to your minister. Maybe you want it secular. Maybe you want it spiritual but not theist. Yes, you can ask a blessing upon a meal that would appeal even to an atheist. I once did a non-theistic "Christening" of a child, and used the word "guide-parents" instead of godparents. If your officiant is comfortable with it, do what is most meaningful to you.

Theme

Having the couple and the officiant on the same page has all sorts of benefits. There are two themes to consider — that of the couple and that of the ceremony.

As a minister, I try to get to know the couple. How did they meet? How long have they been an item? How long have they been engaged? Do they have children, either separately from previous relationships or together? Do they want children? This may give me an idea of how to approach the ceremony. Should I speak of uniting two families, or perhaps leave out any reference to children?

Dig deeper. I ask the couple to give a theme to their story. Is it them against the world? Are they the couple no one expected to last? Are they on a journey to see the world, overcome their past, or is it all about making a home for soulmates? Every "sermon" (see back of book) should reflect their unique relationship. A good officiant will work that into the ceremony, or at least not word anything contradictory to their life goals and feelings.

As for the theme of the wedding, is it formal or informal? Should the officiant wear a tux? Is a clerical collar acceptable? Maybe the officiant has a shirt that will match, or at least not conflict, with the color of the bridal party's attire. There's a reason most ministers wear black!

Maybe they have a matching boutonniere or corsage for the officiant. Maybe it will be all in camo for a hunter or military theme. Believe it or not, you can get a clerical shirt or yarmulke in camouflage. I once performed a Halloween-themed wedding and dressed up as Death. Not something usually appropriate, but it went perfectly with 'Morticia and Gomez' pledging their lives (afterlives?) to each other. But you won't know if you don't discuss it.

The License & Certificate

The process isn't hard, but it must be understood. You need a license to get married, and then get the certificate afterward. The couple goes to a municipal clerk's office for a marriage license. Whatever it may entail, they will explain to you.

I cannot speak of other places, but as an example, in New York, you can go any municipality and get a marriage license. It is only good for 30 days, so don't get it too far beforehand. You also don't have to get married in the place you got the license — anywhere in the state will do.

After the ceremony, the license must be signed by the officiant and two witnesses. They are usually the Maid of Honor and Best Man, or parents, but could be anyone. It must then be mailed, by the officiant, the next business day or two to the place it was given from. The license itself will include instructions.

Depending on the city, town, or village, it may take a few days or several weeks to receive the marriage certificate.

If you are going out of the country, there may be confusion over identification not matching your legal name. However, that's a common occurrence, so a reasonable amount of documentation should ensure getting to your honeymoon and back.

The minister may also produce a certificate of his own for you to display. Though not a legal document, it can be a beautiful memento. This is also useful in cases where there is more than one ceremony, such as a formal one after an elopement. This can keep the family happy if the civil ceremony is a secret.

As a minister, I ask the couple to give me the licence at the rehearsal, and I guard it with my life. I bring with me a fancy pen (unless they have one of their own they want to use). The reason is not just being classy, but that the photographer will often take a picture of it being signed by the witnesses. Find a nice location — a fancy table or something else suitable for photos. The best time to do this is when the receiving line is done receiving the guests, and just before more photos are taken.

The Officiant

Since this book is for couples AND officiants, let's start with choosing an officiant. If you're just looking for a piece of paper to make your union legal, a town official may perform the ceremony and even supply witnesses if you need them. And there's always Elvis at a Vegas chapel. But if you're planning a whole wedding with guests and invitations, you have to find someone to do the service.

The most obvious choice is a member of clergy. They should be able to guide you in how the service is conducted and what options are available. Some denominations will not perform an outdoor wedding, or anywhere else that is not previously consecrated. But not everyone belongs to a faith community, or wants to have their wedding at their church. Some people are technically registered at a parish but aren't "in good standing" for various reasons. Or maybe you want to have a wedding at a church you don't belong to, or one of the members isn't of the same faith. You have to find out the rules about all these things.

Hiring a minister of no particular faith or tradition, or at least non-denominational, is common. Some have a lot of experience, and may allow for venues and options you couldn't do otherwise.

Lastly, you can have it done by someone you know, even if they are not a minister. In the United States, the government generally can't argue over who is and is not a minister*, so all that is required is to have some affiliation with some organization that you can be registered with.

This is the old "mail order minister" concept, but is now online instead of in the back of the newspaper. Organizations have been set up for exactly this purpose, with the philosophy that anyone is entitled to be a minister. The most common is Universal Life Church, but some others are specifically Christian.

If you are not a minister and are asked to perform a wedding, just register with them (or a similar group). Don't feel you are unworthy. A wedding officiant is just a formal witness when performing the ceremony. But take it seriously. ANYONE can make a difference in the world by leading prayer, speaking at funerals, or having a scripture study group. Those are all ministries and don't require a degree in Theology. In many traditions and times in history, ministers and even military chaplains have been chosen by the community without any formal training. And according to Paul of Tarsus, we are all "a priestly people".

Just know your limits. You may not be authorized to perform religious ceremonies of a particular faith, or be recognized as such if you do. Technically, anyone can baptize a child according to Roman Catholicism, but it's frowned upon if not done by a priest or deacon. And if giving advice to those who may need professional help, make it clear to those involved that you are not a licensed counselor — unless you are.

You are also eligible to register as a hospital chaplain. It's a handy ministry if you belong to a membership-oriented organization and wish to comfort members when hospitalized. Your presence may not count against the limit on the number of visitors, and you may be allowed to visit after usual visiting hours.

If the ceremony takes place within the five boroughs of New York City, anyone performing a wedding ceremony is required to register with the NYC City Clerk. This is regardless of the officiant's ordination or licensing. This requirement is rare, but check with the municipality if in doubt.

The Ceremony

The only rule about how to have a wedding is that there are no rules. Well, okay, there are legal requirements. In most places, there must be two witnesses other than the officiant, and each person must clearly declare they enter freely into marriage to the other. There is usually a pronouncement at the end, such as "By the power vested in me by the State of ..." but apart from legal paperwork, there's really nothing else.

Although anything goes, most wedding ceremonies in America today follow a general, familiar form. The basic elements are as follows, and roughly in this order, but don't have to be:

- Seating of guests
- Procession of the Bride's Maids
- Procession of the Bride, giving away the Bride
- Welcome
- One or more readings, a short sermon
- Statement of intentions
- Blessing of the rings
- Exchange of vows and rings

- Prayer over the couple
- Proclamation
- Recession and the formation of a receiving line

Most weddings don't have all of these elements. Many have most of them.

My goal as an officiant is to make a service have enough elements to feel like something was fulfilled — neither rushed nor dragged out. My target is 20 minutes. If people are standing, they won't get fatigued. They won't be looking for a place to sit, or the restrooms, or at their watches. But they will know something memorable and official happened. If the officiant gives some words, let it not be a lengthy sermon. (There's an old saying among preachers that "no one is saved after the first ten minutes of a sermon".) It should be about the couple, or the institution of marriage, or the sacrament of matrimony. Guests don't want to be preached to.

Being light-hearted is important. Solemnity is one thing, but being seriously uptight is too much for what is supposed to be a joyous occasion. The Bride and Groom are sometimes wound up so tight they will burst. An amusing word or two can break the tension, and I have had many couples grateful for it. I might say something like, "If you make me cry, I charge double", or, after asking if anyone objects, quip, "Are you sure?" or express a visible sigh of relief.

A hand on a shoulder can also go a long way.

The couple may need to be reminded that perfection isn't the goal, and the little variety of ways in which things move along make the experience much more human.

Music

There are no limits to what you can do with music. For most ceremonies, I recommend a simple plan — music for the procession and the recession.

You could use one piece of music for the entire procession. Sometimes it is preceded by other music while people are being seated. The main decision to be made is whether you want a special piece to be played just for when the Bride walks down the aisle.

These pieces don't have to be long. Even a three-minute piece is enough for most processions. They move slowly, and the runway may be long, and there may be many people coming down the aisle, but you would be surprised how little time it takes. If anything, you need to fade out or finish out the music before moving on.

Perfect timing for the recessional music is when the whole "you may kiss the Bride" thing happens. Just let the music run out after the party exits the space.

The question is, what music will you choose? The most traditional pieces are Pachelbel's Canon in D and Wagner's Bridal

Chorus ("Here Comes the Bride"), but these can be done in any style, from orchestral to organ, to piano or string quartet. Let it set whatever mood you are going for. Mendelssohn's Wedding March makes a good recessional at the end, in my opinion.

Modern music is perfectly acceptable. In fact, the couple's favorite song, or whatever pop (or country, etc.) song is currently in fashion for weddings, is perfect for when the bridal party departs.

Recorded music is the norm these days, but one or more pieces may be performed by live musicians. You may wish to have something performed as an interlude. It's a perfect time for that one relative with a decent voice who wants to use that talent as a special gift. You can work it in around the time of the readings.

If recorded, make sure someone competent runs it. It could be a boom box or a wifi speaker, but they should have control over fading in and out and switching tracks without a hitch. I recommend having all the music put in one place, even numbered as tracks if possible. There should be no problem going to the next piece without looking for it.

Also, consider the space. The outdoors requires more amplification, and ideally, the officiant should have a microphone. Most of the sound will get lost in the trees if you don't work it out, and people not in the front row won't hear you. However, this might not be necessary in a hall or small church. Test the sound ahead of time, especially if not using a professional DJ.

The Wedding Party

There are countless ways to organize who is standing up, processing in, or waiting at the altar or dais. What you ultimately decide is a matter of tradition or preference.

Customarily, there is at least someone acting as a maid (or matron) of honor for the bride and a best man for the groom. There could be more than one of each, or others simply in the party. Typically, the bride and the women are to the right (when facing the congregation), and the groom and the men are to the left. (This could be explained as the "Mary side" and the "Joseph side" of a Catholic Church). The Best Man and Maid of Honor are right next to the Groom and Bride, respectively.

They should be lined up at the front of the ceremonial area. The line is usually a curve, bringing the ends closer to the congregation. Make sure they all can be seen by everyone, and good photos can be taken.

The ring-bearer or flower girl(s) are usually seated off to the side. Children tend not to stand well in place for the time it takes to perform the service.

There may be a ring-bearer, but the real rings are almost never on the ring pillow. If one is used, a fake ring (or rings) is attached to it and then hidden away once passed to the officiant. That way, the real rings can't get lost or switched by mistake in the shuffle.

I refuse to hold onto them as an officiant. At my first wedding, that of a dear friend and their love, I was handed both of them. I tucked them into my shirt pocket and when I checked again, I could only find one! We searched the room and the grounds until I discovered that the bride's ring was nested perfectly inside the groom's. I had it all along, and we can joke about it now, but it was nearly a coronary event!

The exchange of rings seems straightforward, but can get confusing if not rehearsed. For example, who has what ring? The Best Man should have the Bride's ring and the Maid of Honor should have the Groom's — they are to be passed across to each other. It is ideal for these two people to keep track of them.

The Procession

A procession isn't required, but it's rare not to have one. And there's no right way to process. But some ways are much more common than others. Here's a rundown.

The Groom is almost always waiting with the officiant in front of the altar or dais. The groomsman may already be in place, or may accompany the women up the aisle. However, the Best Man is in place if the Maid of Honor walks without him as an escort.

Sometimes, the men of the party escort the parents of the Bride and Groom to their places in the congregation (usually the front row) before the rest of the procession begins.

The order or procession varies. The extra bridesmaids (with or without an escort) come before the maid of honor, and the bride comes down the aisle last. If there are children strewing flowers or carrying the ring, they may go anywhere in the line before the Bride — first, before the Maid of Honor, or last.

Everyone should walk normally, but slowly. There is no need to do that odd stepping from times past unless it appeals to you. Even then, I suggest that only the bride do it. You can't walk slow enough! You will always be faster than you think, and the music won't run out. I promise.

I try to stagger the people processing such that the next one goes after the one in front of them after they make it halfway up the aisle.

However, after everyone else, the aisle belongs to the Bride alone (and the presenter, if there is one). Only after everyone else is in place should the bride enter and begin — WHEN THEY ARE READY. This is often where the music switches, playing the end of the first piece or fading it out, then beginning the new piece.

Presenting the Bride

Anyone can give away the Bride — a parent, stepparent, sibling, mentor. It could even be a parent AND stepparent sharing the duty.

The minister may ask who offers the Bride's hand in marriage, or they could be passed to the Groom without words as the music plays. But it starts with the Bride and the one presenting them just out of sight, waiting to enter. They may immediately follow the processional party, or wait until they have the runway all to themselves.

I recommend the latter, as the Bride's entrance usually marks the time everyone stands. And it also puts the timing on her terms. She comes when she comes. If she needs a last hug or some calming words, everyone else can wait. It's not like they can start without her!

Handing off the Bride can be a simple as walking up and letting go. I teach the person presenting the meaningful (and photogenic) process I call "Hug, Shake, and Pass". In other words, they hug the Bride, shake the Groom's hand, and then place her hand in his. (I'm not crying, you are!) If you are an officiant, go through this with them. Some fathers or other parent figures are as emotionally stressed as the couple and need to know they'll be alright.

After the pass, the presenter then retires to the side. Make sure beforehand that there is a place for them to sit.

It's that simple. It may seem like an antiquated practice, but if it's meaningful to you, make the most of it.

Readings

R eadings are a matter of preference and tradition. For example, a Catholic Liturgy of the Word involves an Old Testament Reading, a Psalm, a New Testament reading, and one from the Gospels. Even for a Christian wedding, that's a bit much outside of a regular Sunday service.

You can choose any readings you please, taking into account the restrictions or requirements of the religious tradition and officiant you have chosen. Otherwise, it can include scripture from any faith, or secular works — poems, excerpts from books, Shakespeare, nearly anything. Keep in mind that some commonly used readings may seem sexist today, and some translations use words that are more or less appropriate for the occasion.

One or two is enough. Sometimes, these are used to directly involve certain family or friends who want to have a part to play. But make sure the officiant is ready to do them instead, as many of those asked chicken out beforehand. As an officiant, I give the reader a large-print, by-itself copy, and keep an extra tucked in whatever book I hold at the altar. I avoid people reading from a large tome, where they have to find their place, and often their eyeglasses. If we want them to look like they are reading from a huge volume, I have a copy sitting on it for them to use.

For suggested readings, see the appendix at the back of this book.

Vows

When considering vows, go over the wording beforehand. Some versions include an oath to "obey" their husband, and this doesn't fare well with most people today.

You should also work out how you want your names to be said. It could be formal with middle names and all ("James Frederic Smith"), or a nickname and last name ("Jimmy Smith"), or anything in between. Using what you call yourself, or what other people call you, is acceptable even if it doesn't exactly match the name on your birth certificate or driver's license.

Vows are usually exchanged either by having the groom and then bride repeat words of commitment, or the officiant asks them and they each respond "I do".

This is when rings are exchanged. The process is simple, but easy to get tangled.

As an officiant, I start by signaling to the Best Man to give the Groom the ring. Remember, the Best Man has the Bride's ring and the Maid of Honor has the Groom's. The ring is slipped onto the finger partway. The vows are repeated or affirmed, and the ring is slipped all the way into place. To not get mixed up, I tell them to use their left hand to grab the other's left hand, using their right hand to place the ring. Then the roles are reversed. It all seems obvious, but not so easy under pressure — unless you practice it.

Many couples want to write their own vows, but this is a little tricky. The Bride may read something typed or written out on both sides of a sheet of paper. The Groom may have a handful of words scribbled on a napkin. That's okay! You can even joke about it beforehand. The important thing is have something to say, and say it.

Technically, what couples write are not usually "vows". They may recollect how they fell in love or what they mean to each other. The officiant probably won't even be aware of what they will say until that moment. What I do is, after each reads or says what they need to, I have them place the ring after a very brief vow of affirmation.

And for the record, "YES" or any other affirmation is as good as any "I do".

The Rehearsal

The rehearsal can make or break how smoothly the ceremony will go. It can be a time to catch up with relatives, and there may be a meal afterward, but set aside an hour to really go through it. It shouldn't take more than half an hour, but it's like herding cats. Sometimes key people are late, and you have to decide to wait or use placeholders. Sometimes you have to go through details with people who can't be there at another time, even just before the wedding.

Besides finding out any potential problems with a dry run, it also makes the experience a little familiar to the participants. That means they won't feel like their in an alien environment, or doing something unfamiliar for the first time. It's a huge peace of mind.

NEVER skimp on having a thorough rehearsal.

When

The first consideration is how close to the day of the ceremony it should be held. Sometimes it absolutely must be the evening before, as the key players aren't coming into town before then. If availability isn't an issue, then even a week before is fine.

Where

Ideally, it should be done in the exact location you plan to have it. If you are planning to have it outdoors with an indoor contingency, run through it outdoors, but also run through it indoors if you can. Seriously, don't trust the weather. I had a Bride insist there would be no rain on her special day. That was the weekend we got the back end of Hurricane Sandy.

The main reason to practice in any space you may use is that you don't know the limitations of the space until you try using it. Will pillars be obscuring half the bridal party? Is there a tripping hazard that may make procession difficult?

I performed my sister's wedding at a tavern. During the rehearsal, they planned to walk into the room, cut behind some seating to a raised platform, then step off the platform and come down the aisle. I told them they had to be kidding. The Bride, Groom, and Maid of Honor were all legally blind. I asked a server if they ever did weddings there and how they usually did it. She said they only ever did "Tony and Tina's Wedding", a performance of actors with audience participation in the form of a comical wedding and reception. We did it that way. If in doubt, ask the people of the establishment!

Find Your Places

Here's a counterintuitive trick when rehearsing: START AT THE END.

It's easiest to know where you're going if you line up where you will be. Figure out exactly where everyone will stand during the ceremony. This will make it much easier to figure out how they will process at the beginning and take those places. Then practice how you will leave.

The couple and the officiant form a triangle with the preacher, as explained more below. Look at the chapter "The Wedding Party" for details or placing the rest of the party.

The Bride and Groom, of course, will stop for their photogenic shot, ring hand placed over ring hand so both rings can be seen. Practice that, because it's awkward.

After a dramatic pause and the music begins, they switch to holding hands more naturally and go down the aisle. They should have a spot outside the room or area where they can line up with the rest of the wedding party and receive the guests.

After they are just about out of the room, the Best Man escorts the Maid of Honor down the aisle. When halfway down, the next groomsman (if any) escorts the next bridesmaid, and so on. Even if explained and rehearsed, the officiant will probably need to direct traffic, signaling each couple to go at the right time.

When everyone is out the back, sometimes the officiant will need to signal the congregation that it's okay to leave and go congratulate the couple.

After rehearsing this, everyone will be in back, and they can decide the best way to line up so everyone gets hugs and handshakes. The Bride and Groom should be at the beginning or end of the line.

Go Through the Ceremony

Already in the area they need to be, the wedding party should practice processing into the places they just came from. If they haven't decided already, this is the time the order of procession must be set. Take heed of the chapter "Procession" and be as sure as you can be about how you want it. Doing something different than what you practice will increase confusion when it's for real.

Look back at the chapter "Presenting the Bride" for the nitty-gritty on that.

The officiant is between and behind the couple. When the officiant is talking, the couple should make room for him to move forward a bit, between them, so he can be heard and seen. During the exchange of rings and any time they should be close or holding hands, the officiant backs up out of the way.

Anyone doing a reading should practice it then and there, if they can. Give them advice and encouragement. Make sure they understand that no matter how slow they think they are speaking, it will be much faster. This is particularly important in a large room or church because of the echo.

Go through and explain anything that will happen, including special ceremonies or rituals (see appendix). When the practice ceremony is finished, you can then practice recessing again if you like. Do it all over if you feel you need to. But again, perfection isn't the point. If people generally follow the plan comfortably, it will all be fine.

For Children: Assign a Catcher

If children are involved in the procession, have someone ready to bring them off to the side once they finish strewing flowers or handing a ring-pillow to the minister. I cannot stress this enough: it CANNOT BE NO ONE IN PARTICULAR. Someone specific must commit to "catching" and watching them during the ceremony, often a grandparent. Otherwise, there will be confusion or even competition. But pick someone reliable. At one wedding, the catcher wasn't paying attention, and the toddler ring-bearer came dangerously close to some stairs.

The Big Day

I'm not really in charge of a wedding I may perform, but neither is anyone else unless you have a wedding planner. But I try to instill in everyone involved, and make it clear at rehearsal, one thing: Anything that happens the day of the wedding should fall under the category of NOT THE COUPLE'S PROBLEM. Everyone else should run interference for them. Unless there is a decision that absolutely must be made by the couple, they shouldn't be bothered.

The Maid of Honor and Best Man tend to be charged with caring for their respective half of the couple. Unashamedly, let's call it babysitting. They should be able to just breathe and be reassured by those around them.

As an officiant, I try to get the paperwork (marriage license) at the rehearsal so they don't have to keep track of it. I make sure to talk to the photographer (see that chapter) if I haven't already. I greet people, and if needed, "warm up the crowd". To break the tension, I've told jokes to the wedding party. And I try to be the Groom's personal support during moments when it may be just us up front, waiting to begin.

Whatever happens will happen. Deal with things as you need to, but leave as little to chance as you can by planning beforehand. Leave as little to the last minute as possible. If something isn't right, you may have to let it go. You may not even remember it years later, or remember that it turned out fine anyway.

Photography

C apturing a moment like a wedding is really important to some, even if it doesn't seem important to others. You don't want to be without some *good* photos. The truth is, even with the fanciest smartphones, you are probably never going to get something worthy of being framed without paying someone a professional rate.

A dear friend decided to go with everyone being given disposable cameras (back in the day of actual film). Apart from all the awkward, under-the-table shots taken by kids, they got about a thousand images. Not a single one was particularly good. It would have been a fun addition to the event, but not a substitute.

Not all professional photographers are created equal, either. Some do not have experience in events, other than maybe sports. Ones who really know what they are doing will be like ninjas — you won't remember them even being there. They may wear all black to move like shadows in the background. They won't crawl up to people for the up-the-nose shots. They won't block people's views or invade the space around the officiant.

Some shots can be pre-planned. As an officiant, I rehearse the couple to turn around after being announced, and pause, holding hands in a way that both rings can be seen. The photographer will be waiting for that money shot. If they don't get it, they know they can recreate a close-up of the hands later.

Let them know about the signing of the license if it is to be photographed, and tell them you want it done after the receiving line is finished, before they take more photos.

I've never had a problem with photographers, but I always insist on talking to them beforehand. Sure, I go over the 'rules of the ninja' as I call them, but in a very diplomatic way. I tell them we will try to place everyone in a way they can move around the room without crossing between people. I tell them about particular times they may want to get a shot, reassuring them we can recreate them if need be.

The Reception

The wedding may be held at the reception hall, or it could be at some other place. It may be right away, or a few hours after the ceremony, to take photos, possibly at a third location.

For some, the reception IS the wedding, or the essence of the festivities. This is where people can be themselves. But there is still some structure. Here is a typical itinerary.

After everyone is settled and the wedding party is back from photos and such, their entrance is announced. Usually, the groomsmen and bridesmaids enter the hall one of each at a time. The couple enters last, usually "introduced for the first time" by the DJ or master of ceremonies. (This is why I don't use words that "introduce" the couple at the end of the ceremony.)

Like the wedding procession, there may be different music used for the couple from the rest of the party.

The officiant should be told if they are welcome at the reception, and if they should bring their spouse. If they are giving grace over the meal, they should find out when. They may work it out with the DJ to borrow their microphone. The best time is before everyone sits, but often it is done sometime during, or even after the meal.

This may be obvious to some, but not everyone has been to a wedding or reception and is unsure of seating. The head table is ordinarily reserved for the wedding party — those who "stood up" and likely had matching attire. Just like at the ceremony, it's the Bride and Groom in the middle, the Best Man and Maid of Honor flanking them, and the others to the sides. If there is room, those standing up may have their spouses seated next to them.

The Best Man and Maid of Honor will speak and give a toast. This is usually done after dinner, but could be at any time. Others may be welcome to speak. Knowing ahead of time is best, but spontaneous expressions of affection may add to the special day.

Cutting the cake is usually done at dessert time. It should be protected from children (of any age), and the photographer should be ready. One important note: Smooshing cake in your spouse's face should be consensual!

Most receptions have dancing, with the first dance traditionally going to the Bride with their father. The Groom may dance with his mother as well, or they may swap, dancing with their in-laws.

If there will be a tossing of the bouquet, plan when and how. It may be at the end of the ceremony, but if done with the garter as well, after the dancing starts is a good time. Decide if you want children to have a chance, if they are invited at all. Sometimes things can get awkward if certain people get the bouquet and garter.

There may be other family traditions expected, but it's ultimately the couple's choice. But be prepared for surprises. And forgiveness is reasonable if the couple sneaks out early to start their honeymoon.

No Regrets

L et me share with you a life hack I use to avoid regrets. It in-volves time travel. Imagine yourself years from now. What would be your greatest regret? What would you wish you had more time to do or have done differently?

Think of your wedding, so many years ago. What is it you wish you had done? Did you fail to do a family tradition you thought was too silly at the time? Did you skimp on really good photos? Did you wish you could go back in time and ask your best friend to sing?

It doesn't matter how outlandish or crazy something might have seemed. Do you wish it had been a fond memory? What fin-ishing touches did you forget to do, and is now too late? (Take a look at some of the ceremonies in the back of this book for exam-ples of how people make their wedding extra-special.)

Now come back to the present. Will everything be as you will someday have hoped it was? You don't need to apologize to any-one for your dreams. In the end, you may only have to apologize to yourself.

This doesn't mean do every possible thing that comes to mind. It's just brainstorming. But some things may hit you like a cannonball. Some detail may become a cherished memory, forever. Discuss this thoroughly with your partner.

And use this "trick" from time to time as you grow older together.

YOUR SPOUSE'S INSTRUCTION MANUAL

Over time, we get to know the ins and outs of living with someone as a couple. But sometimes we need reminding that differences and preferences aren't a battle to be fought. It's the lay of the land in your relationship.

That is why I created a one-page worksheet called "Your Spouse's Instruction Manual". When working with couples, I tell them each to fill out a copy and give it to the other person. They can pin it to a corkboard in their personal space or keep it in their sock drawer. They may see it as a dear memento years from now.

If you do this exercise, sit down and give your responses to each other. There are no right or wrong answers. You may or may not refer to it in the future. And some of these answers may change over time, or can be negotiated in practice. The point is to have an awareness and build tolerance and understanding.

A printable version is available at OtherFlock.Org. The basic form of it is below.

Name _____
{Circle the answer that fits best for you.}

- When I am upset, I most want you to (fix the problem / give me sympathy / leave me alone).
- When we have a disagreement, it is hardest for me to (deal with it right then and there / put off resolving it).
- I feel most loved when you (give me things to show you care / say you love me / give me physical attention / spend time with me)
- What I fear the most is (losing you / misunderstanding each other / being alone).
- What I want most from life is to be (happy / secure / healthy).
- For fidelity, I draw the line at you (spending too much time with someone else / spending time with someone else alone / having romantic involvement / not coming home).
- When I sleep, I'm usually (too hot / too cold / just right).
- Air conditioning is (wonderful / uncomfortable / alright).
- I prefer sex (in the morning / evening or night / during the day / at no particular time).
- I prefer sex to be initiated by (me / you / either of us).
- I prefer you to be (aggressive / passive / passive or aggressive depending on my mood).
- I am best when I (am doing several things at once / focus on one thing at a time).
- When deciding what to do together, I prefer you to (be decisive for me / support my decision / be decisive when I can't).

- I'd prefer children to be disciplined by (you / me / whichever of us is at hand).
- When meeting new people, I want to (be introduced / introduce myself / be invisible).
- Other:

LIFE VALUES WORKSHEET

This worksheet is about values and trust. These should be done separately from one another and then shared. There are no right or wrong answers. Comparing and discussing builds the awareness you need for your lifelong journey.

We all place more or less value on various things. We can better live and get along with those who share most of our core values. But no two people are alike. This gives you a sort of roadmap of what to expect. Do you both have the same goals now? Will your goals be very different later? This can be worked out before it becomes a reason for conflict. You can be ready to deal with such things openly.

The second half of the worksheet focuses on trust. Trust here isn't about honesty or dishonesty, but more a matter of confidence. Maybe one of you isn't good at balancing the checkbook or is not confident in making medical decisions. These can be worked out. But PLEASE try not to be offended if your spouse doesn't trust you to handle certain things. They may see your strengths and weaknesses differently than you do. Maybe they are right. Most often, you know there's good reason for them not to trust you with some things. That's okay.

If you have very different answers, that's GOOD. It means you can more easily divide responsibilities in a way that makes sense.

A printable version is available at OtherFlock.Org. The basic form of it is below.

Name _____

How important do you think the following are / will be in your relationship with each other, on a scale of 0-5?

{There are TWO answers for each one. First rate current importance, and then rate how important you think these thigns will be later in life.}

- Your Family
- Their Family
- Sex
- Children
- Financial Security
- Social Life
- Health
- Luxuries
- Religion
- Recreation

How comfortable do you feel about your spouse making decisions in the following areas, on a scale of 0-5?

- Household Finances
- Holiday with Families

- Where you live
- Birth Control
- Child Care & Upbringing
- Legal Transactions
- Medical Decisions
- Major Purchases
- Scheduling Family

APPENDIX: READINGS

Bible Passages

There are many suitable passages in scripture for most religious traditions. Here are some of the more common ones from the Judeo-Christian Bible. Translations may vary, so feel free to compare and find one that speaks to you.

Old Testament

Genesis 2:18-24

The LORD God said, "It is not good for the man to be alone. I will make a helper suitable for him." Now the LORD God had formed out of the ground all the beasts of the field and all the birds of the air. He brought them to the man to see what he would name them; and whatever the man called each living creature, that was its name. So the man gave names to all the livestock, the birds of the air and all the beasts of the field. But for Adam no suitable helper was found. So the LORD God caused the man to fall into a deep sleep; and while he was sleeping, he took one of the man's ribs and closed up the place with flesh. Then the LORD God made a woman from the rib he had taken out of the man, and he brought her to the man.

The man said, "This is now bone of my bones and flesh of my flesh; she shall be called 'woman,' for she was taken out of man." For this reason a man will leave his father and mother and be united to his wife, and they will become one flesh.

Ecclesiastes 4:9-12

Two are better than one, because they have a good return for their work: If one falls down, his friend can help him up. But pity the man who falls and has no one to help him up!
Also, if two lie down together, they will keep warm. But how can one keep warm alone?
Though one may be overpowered, two can defend themselves. A cord of three strands is not quickly broken.

Gospels

Matthew 19:4-6

Haven't you read," he replied, "that at the beginning the Creator 'made them male and female,' and said, 'For this reason a man will leave his father and mother and be united to his wife, and the two will become one flesh'? So they are no longer two, but one. Therefore what God has joined together, let man not separate."

Mark 10:6-9

But at the beginning of creation God 'made them male and female.' For this reason a man will leave his father and mother and be united to his wife, and the two will become one flesh.' So they are no longer two, but one. Therefore what God has joined together, let man not separate.

Matthew 7:24-27

Therefore everyone who hears these words of mine and puts them into practice is like a wise man who built his house on the rock. The rain came down, the streams rose, and the winds blew and beat against that house; yet it did not fall, because it had its foundation on the rock. But everyone who hears these words of mine and does not put them into practice is like a foolish man who built his house on sand. The rain came down, the streams rose, and the winds blew and beat against that house, and it fell with a great crash."

New Testament Espistles

1 Corinthians 7

The husband should fulfill his marital duty to his wife, and likewise the wife to her husband. The wife's body does not belong to her alone but also to her husband. In the same way, the husband's body does not belong to him alone but also to his wife. Do not deprive each other except by mutual consent and for a time, so that you may devote yourselves to prayer. Then come together again so that Satan will not tempt you because of your lack of self-control. I say this as a concession, not as a command. I wish that all men were as I am. But each man has his own gift from God; one has this gift, another has that.

...

But if the unbeliever leaves, let him do so. A believing man or woman is not bound in such circumstances; God has called us to live in peace. How do you know, wife, whether you will save your husband? Or, how do you know, husband, whether you will save your wife?

Ephesians 5:22-33

Wives, submit to your husbands as to the Lord. For the husband is the head of the wife as Christ is the head of the church, his body, of which he is the Savior. Now as the church submits to Christ, so also wives should submit to their husbands in everything. Husbands, love your wives, just as Christ loved the church and gave himself up for her to make her holy, cleansing her by the washing with water through the word, and to present her to himself as a radiant church, without stain or wrinkle or any other blemish, but holy and blameless. In this same way, husbands ought to love their wives as their own bodies. He who loves his wife loves himself. After all, no one ever hated his own body, but he feeds and cares for it, just as Christ does the church-for we are members of his body. "For this reason a man will leave his father and mother and be united to his wife, and the two will become one flesh." This is a profound mystery-but I am talking about Christ and the church. However, each one of you also must love his wife as he loves himself, and the wife must respect her husband.

Colossians 3:18,19

Wives, submit to your husbands, as is fitting in the Lord. Husbands, love your wives and do not be harsh with them.

Hebrews 13:4-7

Marriage should be honored by all, and the marriage bed kept pure, for God will judge the adulterer and all the sexually immoral. Keep your lives free from the love of money and be content with what you have, because God has said,
"Never will I leave you; never will I forsake you." So we say with confidence, "The Lord is my helper; I will not be afraid. What can man do to me?"
Remember your leaders, who spoke the word of God to you. Consider the outcome of their way of life and imitate their faith.

Romans 12: 9-21

Love must be sincere. Hate what is evil; cling to what is good. Be devoted to one another in brotherly love. Honor one another above yourselves. Never be lacking in zeal, but keep your spiritual fervor, serving the Lord. Be joyful in hope, patient in affliction, faithful in prayer. Share with God's people who are in need. Practice hospitality. Bless those who persecute you; bless and do not curse. Rejoice with those who rejoice; mourn with those who mourn. Live in harmony with one another. Do not be proud, but be willing to associate with people of low position. Do not be conceited.

Do not repay anyone evil for evil. Be careful to do what is right in the eyes of everybody. If it is possible, as far as it depends on you, live at peace with everyone. Do not take revenge, my friends, but leave room for God's wrath, for it is written: "It is mine to avenge; I will repay," says the Lord. On the contrary:

"If your enemy is hungry, feed him; if he is thirsty, give him something to drink. In doing this, you will heap burning coals on his head."

Do not be overcome by evil, but overcome evil with good.

1 Corinthians 13:1-13

If I speak in the tongues of men and of angels, but have not love, I am only a resounding gong or a clanging cymbal. If I have the gift of prophecy and can fathom all mysteries and all knowledge, and if I have a faith that can move mountains, but have not love, I am nothing. If I give all I possess to the poor and surrender my body to the flames, but have not love, I gain nothing. Love is patient, love is kind. It does not envy, it does not boast, it is not proud. It is not rude, it is not self-seeking, it is not easily angered, it keeps no record of wrongs. Love does not delight in evil but rejoices with the truth. It always protects, always trusts, always hopes, always perseveres.

Love never fails. But where there are prophecies, they will cease; where there are tongues, they will be stilled; where there is knowledge, it will pass away. For we know in part and we prophesy in part, but when perfection comes, the imperfect disappears. When I was a child, I talked like a child, I thought like a child, I reasoned like a child. When I became a man, I put childish ways behind me. Now we see but a poor reflection as in a mirror; then we shall see face to face. Now I know in part; then I shall know fully, even as I am fully known.

And now these three remain: faith, hope and love. But the greatest of these is love.

1 John 4:9-12

This is how God showed his love among us: He sent his one and only Son into the world that we might live through him. This is love: not that we loved God, but that he loved us and sent his Son as an atoning sacrifice for our sins. Dear friends, since God so loved us, we also ought to love one another. No one has ever seen God; but if we love one another, God lives in us and his love is made complete in us.

Colossians 3:12-17

Therefore, as God's chosen people, holy and dearly loved, clothe yourselves with compassion, kindness, humility, gentleness and patience. Bear with each other and forgive whatever grievances you may have against one another. Forgive as the Lord forgave you. And over all these virtues put on love, which binds them all together in perfect unity. Let the peace of Christ rule in your hearts, since as members of one body you were called to peace. And be thankful. Let the word of Christ dwell in you richly as you teach and admonish one another with all wisdom, and as you sing psalms, hymns and spiritual songs with gratitude in your hearts to God. And whatever you do, whether in word or deed, do it all in the name of the Lord Jesus, giving thanks to God the Father through him.

Other Readings

Robert Fulghum - 'Union'

You have known each other from the first glance of acquaintance to this point of commitment. At some point, you decided to marry. From that moment of yes, to this moment of yes, indeed, you have been making commitments in an informal way. All of those conversations that were held in a car, or over a meal, or during long walks – all those conversations that began with, "When we're married", and continued with "I will" and "you will" and "we will" – all those late night talks that included "someday" and "somehow" and "maybe" – and all those promises that are unspoken matters of the heart. All these common things, and more, are the real process of a wedding.

The symbolic vows that you are about to make are a way of saying to one another, "You know all those things that we've promised, and hoped, and dreamed – well, I meant it all, every word." Look at one another and remember this moment in time. Before this moment you have been many things to one another – acquaintance, friend, companion, lover, dancing partner, even teacher, for you have learned much from one another these past few years. Shortly you shall say a few words that will take you across a threshold of life, and things between you will never quite be the same.

For after today you shall say to the world – This is my husband. This is my wife.

A letter of Samuel Clemens (Mark Twain) to Olivia Langdon, his fiancée

This will be the mightiest day in the history of our lives, the holiest, and the most generous toward us both — for it makes of two fractional lives a whole;

It gives to two purposeless lives a work,

And doubles the strength of each whereby to perform it;

It gives to two questioning natures a reason for living,

And something to live for;

It will give a new gladness to the sunshine,

A new fragrance to the flowers,

A new beauty to the earth, a new mystery to life;

And it will give a new revelation to love,

And a new depth to sorrow, a new impulse to worship.

On this day the scales will fall from our eyes and we shall look upon a new world.

"Marriage Joins Two People in the Circle of Its Love" by Edmund O'Neill

Marriage is a commitment to life, the best that two people can find and bring out in each other. It offers opportunities for sharing and growth that no other relationship can equal. It is a physical and an emotional joining that is promised for a lifetime.

Within the circle of its love, marriage encompasses all of life's most important relationships. A wife and a husband are each other's best friend, confidant, lover, teacher, listener, and critic. And there may come times when one partner is heartbroken or ailing, and the love of the other may resemble the tender caring of a parent for a child.

Marriage deepens and enriches every facet of life. Happiness is fuller, memories are fresher, commitment is stronger, even anger is felt more strongly, and passes away more quickly.
Marriage understands and forgives the mistakes life is unable to avoid.

It encourages and nurtures new life, new experiences, and new ways of expressing a love that is deeper than life.

When two people pledge their love and care for each other in marriage, they create a spirit unique unto themselves which binds them closer than any spoken or written words. Marriage is a promise, a potential made in the hearts of two people who love each other and takes a lifetime to fulfil.

"The Art of Marriage" by Wilferd A. Peterson

... In the art of marriage the little things are the big things...
It is never being too old to hold hands.
It is remembering to say "I love you" at least once a day.
It is never going to sleep angry.

It is at no time taking the other for granted; the courtship should not end with the honeymoon, it should continue through all the years.

It is having a mutual sense of values and common objectives.

It is standing together facing the world.

It is forming a circle of love that gathers in the whole family.

It is doing things for each other, not in the attitude of duty or sacrifice, but in the spirit of joy.

It is speaking words of appreciation and demonstrating gratitude in thoughtful ways.

It is not looking for perfection in each other.

It is cultivating flexibility, patience, understanding and a sense of humour.

It is having the capacity to forgive and forget.

It is giving each other an atmosphere in which each can grow.

It is finding room for the things of the spirit.

It is a common search for the good and the beautiful.

It is establishing a relationship in which the independence is equal, dependence is mutual and the obligation is reciprocal.

It is not only marrying the right partner, it is being the right partner. ...

"Blessings for a Marriage" by James Freeman

May your marriage bring you all the exquisite excitements a marriage should bring, and may life grant you also patience, tolerance, and understanding.

May you always need one another — not so much to fill your emptiness as to help you to know your fullness. A mountain needs a valley to be complete; the valley does not make the mountain less, but more; and the valley is more a valley because it has a mountain towering over it. So let it be with you and you.

May you need one another, but not out of weakness.

May you want one another, but not out of lack.

May you entice one another, but not compel one another.

May you embrace one another, but not out encircle one another.

May you succeed in all important ways with one another, and not fail in the little graces.

May you look for things to praise, often say, "I love you!" and take no notice of small faults.

If you have quarrels that push you apart, may both of you hope to have good sense enough to take the first step back.

May you enter into the mystery, which is the awareness of one another's presence - no more physical than spiritual, warm and near when you are side-by-side, and warm and near when you are in separate rooms or even distant cities. May you have happiness, and may you find it making one another happy.

May you have love, and may you find it loving one another.

The Art of a Good Marriage by Wilferd Arlan Peterson

The little things are the big things.

It is never being too old to hold hands.

It is remembering to say "I love you" at least once a day.

It is never going to sleep angry.

It is never taking the other for granted; the courtship should not end with the honeymoon, it should continue through all the years.

It is having a mutual sense of values and common objectives.

It is standing together facing the world.

It is forming a circle of love that gathers in the whole family.

It is doing things for each other, not in the attitude of duty or sacrifice, but in the spirit of joy.

It is speaking words of appreciation and demonstrating gratitude in thoughtful ways.

It is not expecting the husband to wear a halo or the wife to have wings of an angel.

It is not looking for perfection in each other.

It is cultivating flexibility, patience, understanding and a sense of humor.

It is having the capacity to forgive and forget.

It is giving each other an atmosphere in which each can grow.

It is finding room for the things of the spirit.

It is a common search for the good and the beautiful.

It is establishing a relationship in which the independence is equal, dependence is mutual and the obligation is reciprocal.

It is not only marrying the right partner, it is being the right partner.

APPENDIX: CEREMONIES

Blessing of Rings

The officiant asks the best man and maid of honor to present the rings. They step in front of the couple, extending their palms (carrying the rings) toward each other. The officiant places his hand above them. The blessing is typically similar to the following words: "We bless these rings, having no beginning and no end, as symbols of eternal Love."

Hand-Fasting

Hand-fasting is an older version of exchanging rings. It would be done instead of an exchange of rings; today it is usually done along with the rings. The couple should have a ribbon or cord on hand, a few feet long. No one wants to trip on it, but it should be long enough to wrap around each other's wrist at least twice.

The officiant does the binding, and has them extend their hands, deciding beforehand what hands they will use. The method I use is to have one of them grasp the end (or near the end) of the cord or ribbon in their palm, wrap around their hand once or twice, then wrap around the other hand, tucking the end into the other person's palm.

It's best to do this after the rings are exchanged (for obvious reasons), and close to the end of the service so they will not have to remove them before walking down the aisle. It can be tricky, so go over this during rehearsal in detail. Don't just talk about how it will be done — practice it until the couple is comfortable and knows what to do.

This often requires explanation for those present who are unfamiliar with this tradition. Therefore, note the following wording at the beginning of this example:

> In addition to the usual ceremony, John and Colleen have chosen to include as part of their wedding ritual the medieval European tradition of hand-fasting, where a ribbon is loosely tied around their joined hands as another way to symbolize their oath of unity.
>
> John and Colleen have shared their love for nearly 6 years. They desire nothing more than to spend the rest of this life together hand in hand.
>
> [Ribbon / cord is placed]
>
> Here before witnesses, they have sworn vows to each other. With this cord, I bind them to the vows that they each have made.
>
> {Wrap the cord loosely around both wrists.}
>
> However, these are not ties that bind. Neither is restricted by the other, the binding held dear by the strength of both their wills.
>
> Please repeat after me ...

"Heart to thee, Soul to thee, Body to thee, Forever and always, So mote it be.*

{"So mote it be" is an Old English version of "so may it be", an equivalent of "Amen"}"

Below is an alternate version of hand fasting:

"Is it also your wish today that your hands be fasted in the ways of old?"

Couple: "It is."

"Remember then as your hands are fasted, these are not the ties that bind…"

{Cords are placed}

"Your Love is strengthened by the vows you have taken. All things material return to the Earth, but the bond your spirits share is destined to ascend to the heavens. May you be forever as one, for you are now as your hearts have always known you to be."

Sand Ceremony

This is not only symbolic, but creates a memento of the occasion. Find a jar of suitable simplicity or decoration to your taste. Procure sand of at least two colors. This should all be set up on a small, secure stand or other place in the ceremonial area.

If done only by the couple, each should take a color and pour it into the common vessel at the same time. The wording to introduce this event can be as follows:

"And now the couple wishes to express their joining in a sand ceremony. May their dreams, hopes, fears, and actions be forever blended into one life and future."

If the wedding also celebrates the uniting of families, as in children, you can have each person (usually the couple as well) take turns pouring in sand, a different color for each person. You may want to choose colors beforehand so there won't be any squabbling at the ceremony! In the case of families, the following wording may be used:

"Now, as a symbol of two families becoming one, the members of this new family will have a sand ceremony, each member contributing their own."

The words "... and voicing what they are grateful for" can be added if you wish for each to do so.

Unity Candle

A single candle stands unlit, with two lit tapers nearby. The candle may be decorated or ornamental, as it will become a memento of the occasion. This should all be set up on a small, secure stand or other place in the ceremonial area. If done outdoors, this may not be a good option considering wind. However, it could be done at the reception.

The officiant may introduce the ceremony by saying, "The couple will now light a candle together to symbolize two living flames becoming one."

Alternately, it can be lit by representatives of the families of the bride and groom, such as parents.

Just be careful! And be aware that there may be a prohibition against open flames in the location you've chosen for the ceremony.

Special Prayer for Married Couples

{Written by the author}

Sometime after the exchange of rings, the officiant asks all married couples to hold hands as they are able. (I say "as they are able" because some spouses may be split between the congregation and the wedding party, and are therefore not near each other.)

"Creator of the Universe, you have given us each other so that we may Love one another as deeply and completely as You have Loved us.

Help us to take the best examples from those who have gone before us, and may our own Love and lives, in all perfection and imperfection, become an example for others.

Bless our unions with the desire to ever grow closer with each moment, so in the end we may be together, and worthy of ultimate Union with You."

Hands Ceremony

The officiant asks the bride and groom to hold and gaze upon each other's hands.

"These are the hands of your best friend, smooth, young and carefree, that are holding yours on your wedding day, as they promise to love and cherish each other through the years, for a lifetime of happiness.

These are the hands that will work alongside yours, as together you build your future.

These are the hands that will love you passionately, and, with the slightest touch, comfort you like no other.

These are the hands that will countless times wipe the tears from your eyes – tears of sorrow, and tears of joy.

These are the hands that will hold you when fear or grief engulfs your heart.

These are the hands that will give you strength and support when you can't do it alone.

These are the hands that, when wrinkled and aged, will still be reaching for yours, still giving you the same unspoken tenderness with just a touch.

May these hands be blessed this day. May they always hold each other. May they have the strength to hang on during the storms of stress and the dark of disillusionment. May they remain tender and gentle as they nurture each other in their wondrous love. May they build a relationship founded in love, and rich in caring. May these hands be healer, protector, shelter, and guide for each other."

Grace & Moment of Silence

{Written by the author}

Lord, we thank you for the food before us, but we are ever more grateful for the opportunity to share company with loved ones in such a happy occasion.

May we be forever near in each other's hearts, even as we safely part at end of day.

We also ask a special blessing on those in the Armed Forces who sacrifice much and are ever-ready to give all for our wishes of Peace and safety of home and humanity.

And so we bow our heads in a moment of silence for those who are unable to be here due to distance or time, remembering all who have gone before us and all who are here in spirit.

{Moment}

Amen.

Hindu Rituals

The following is a somewhat Americanized version of traditions common to Northern India.

Presenting the Bride

Asked three times, "On behalf of the bride's father, I ask the groom: Do you promise you shall never fail her in your pursuit of moral duty, gainful purpose, and passionate love?"

Kanyadaan

And so the groom declares:

"I take your hand in mine, yearning for happiness
I ask you, to live with me, as your husband
Till both of us, with age, grow old
Know this, as I declare, that the Gods
have bestowed your person, upon me
that I may fulfill, my duties of the householder, with you
This I am, That is you
The Heavens I, the Earth you"

Varmala

As the couple exchanges floral garlands, have them say, "Let all the learned persons present here know, we are accepting each other willingly, voluntarily and pleasantly. Our hearts are concordant and united like waters."

Walk the Holy Fire (Saptapadi - the Seven Steps)

The couple walks around a fire (such as a fire pit) seven times, receiving seven blessings.

1.   May this couple be blessed with an abundance of resources and comforts, and be helpful to one another in all ways.

2.   May this couple be strong and complement one another.

3.   May this couple be blessed with prosperity and riches on all levels.

4.   May this couple be eternally happy.

5.   May this couple be blessed with a happy family life.

6.   May this couple live in perfect harmony, true to their personal values and their joint promises.

7.   May this couple always be the best of lifelong friends.

The couple rejoices:

"You have become mine forever. Yes, we have become partners. I have become yours. Hereafter, I cannot live without you. Do not live without me. Let us share the joys. We are word and meaning, united. You are thought and I am sound. May the night be honey-sweet for us. May the morning be honey-sweet for us. May the earth be honey-sweet for us. May the heavens be honey-sweet for us. As the heavens are stable, as the earth is stable, as the mountains are stable, as the whole universe is stable, so may our union be permanently settled."

SAMPLE HOMILIES

Each Wedding is like no other. I never do the same ceremony twice, or the same personal comments that some would call a sermon or homily. They are very short — a few paragraphs at most. But each one has a theme unique to the couple's journey, their history and hopes for the future.

NOTE: These are not given here for wholesale use in other people's ceremonies. They are here for inspirational purposes only. Feel free to borrow themes and ideas, but they were written with the intention that they have never been used for anyone else before, or will be in the future, making the words unique to themselves as a uniquely special gift.

Karen & Ken

This is a tough one. I've known Karen and her sisters since I was 14 years old. And on and off we've lost touch by circumstance, geography, tragedy. But I've held them in my heart as MY sisters. And in my book, that makes Ken family as well, if he'll have me.

But with so much family here, there's a lesson to be learned. I woke up today remembering something my daughter wrote in a blog. "Life is too short to hold back, but too long to say exactly what's on your mind."

So much has been said, so much has been done. Before the couple met, they had full lives of their own, a tapestry of joys and drama. But time is a lens that focuses our soul to see the Joy crystal clear, and the blurry cloudiness of drama fades away.

So if have one wish for Ken and Karen – and for ALL of us who may hold onto the litanies of past hurts by human imperfection: If we find it hard to focus that lens into the past with forgiveness, let us at least focus it into our future. Let us be ready, with each new day, to separate out all that is not Joy, and embrace it in that which matters most – Love.

Dawn & John

One reason for unhappiness in this life is because we look to change others. But what is the opposite of that? Indifference? Resignment? RESENTMENT? No, our other choice is to allow others to change US.

If you want to know if someone truly belongs in your life, ask yourself this question: Do they make me a better person? But then nobody can make someone a better person unless we open our hearts to them – give them permission to change us, and be willing.

Marriage is perhaps the best opportunity to become a better person. We bare our soul to someone, and unconsciously we want to change, to not only become whole, but to love those parts of us we might not love so much ourselves.

NOW, ask yourself if your love for another makes you less selfish. If it doesn't, it isn't Agape, unconditional LOVE. And if you ever feel you aren't living up to those three words you profess, then allow yourselves to change. Take a step toward selflessness, knowing you no longer live for yourself, but for another.

We learned to love and become who we are from our parents, mentors, friends ... let us never stop allowing our love and the love of others to change us for the better. Let us make our children less selfish by our own Love and example.

This is our calling as spouses, as parents, and human beings – children of a Divine Parent. And that is my wish for the couple and all of you here today.

Russell & Gabriele

At a vocational mass when I was young, a new priest read the wrong passage, followed by the Bishop who had to comment. He said, "With ordination does not come perfection."

Well, I'm here to tell you that with a Wedding does not come happiness. That is something you bring with you to this place, in whatever measure you have it, and make it yours together over a lifetime. The burdens of this worldly existence do not change; our sharing of the burdens takes away the heaviness.

And apart from good wishes and a registry, there is no prize, just those things you bring with you. Your experiences, your memories, your dreams, your burdens, your strengths – in matrimony we bring our very selves to each other, without shame or judgment, or keeping score of any kind.

Paul writes to the Colossians (3:13-17) "Bear with each other and forgive whatever grievances you may have against one another. Forgive as the Lord forgave you. And over all these virtues put on love, which binds them all together in perfect unity."

This is the Love to be chosen each new day, and every moment as best we can. But be gentle with yourselves. Forgive yourselves for the times you don't live up to that ideal. There is always a rising up from each fall, and you have each other's strength, now undivided.

Ryan & Rowland

Our reading has a lot of tongue in it {James 3:3}. The lesson is that what we say (or don't say) can make all the difference in the world. It can hide and hurt, but more importantly it can connect us to one another, and in speaking from our hearts allow vulnerability that is necessary for true Love.

There's a lot more to a relationship than verbal communication, but that is the everyday bridge where we meet, face to face. Our words bear a great responsibility, and a kind word at the right time can change not just OUR world, but THE world.

My wish for the couple is for them to never hold back from expressing Love, need, joy, and also fear, anger, hurt. Even if some things can go unsaid, say them. To not talk is to leave room for a guess, a suspicion, and a missed opportunity to understand and heal. And we all need these things, often.

Ryan, Rowland, you've brought new life to each other. Be ready to REnew your life together, again and again with each experience, with each blessed addition to your family and home, and grow together even more in all the journeys of life.

Brad & Liann

Yes! The very meaning of existence and life is the affirmation of creation to itself. But we, as part of creation, are asked this question as well.

Do we answer back Yes?

We don't usually say 'yes' to thin air out of fear of being declared insane, but in each other we have such an opportunity. We say, YES, I love you, YES, I accept you, YES, I do.

It is the constant amidst the tempest, not a fight against it, but an embrace of all that will or could happen, an acceptance that this is where we need to be, who we need to be, therefore unshakable, unalterable.

That special Yes we say to each other at the altar of creation is an affirmation that we accept who we are in each other, our place together in the world, no matter what it brings.

My blessing and hope for Brad and Liann is that their Yes will not shy from the storm of the changes of life, but grow and encompass all of life around them, making even the hardest times a choice of strength in their own unshakable story.

So what do we say in affirmation of this couple's life together? YES!

Bonita & David

This is the first time I've done a "surprise wedding".

But I have a few words that should be of no surprise. The finding of soul mates are not coincidences. They are one way in which the circumstances of life fall into place. Everything we experience brings us to where we are today.

Some events or details seem so unimportant we don't even notice or give them thought. Even some of the hardest times in our lives, moments of pain and sorrow, help make us who we are – not just for ourselves but for each other.

Most of us are grateful only for the good times – the joys, the triumphs, the times everything seems to go right. But my wish for you is to see ALL your times together to be a blessing. The circumstances that brought you together, and here today, continue to shape your lives in a special way.

That is where Faith comes in. It's hard for us as human beings to not want everything to be perfect, but if we could see as God sees, behind the scenes all that must happen just right, then we will realize that maybe everyday life is the greatest Miracle of all.

It is the music of Life, notes heard and unheard, and melodies that only some people can truly share.

My wish for you is to cherish these miracles, your music, through faith in God and each other.

Crystal and Chris

A wise man once said, "Objects in mirror are closer than they appear."

Things that to us seem so afar are often as important as things at hand. We are millions of miles from the sun and yet it gives this pale blue dot, our tiny stone in an endless silver sea, heat and warmth enabling and sustaining our very existence. Even if the moon hides behind clouds, its influence of the tides can be felt.

Do we believe in the axiom "out of sight, out of mind", or does absence make the heart grow fonder?

When the stars align, or by the will and Grace of God, two people can know and hold a subtle thread, a connection across lapses of time and space. A couple that survives such distance doesn't do so casually, or by accident.

My hopes for the couple are that they never count the miles or minutes of those times when they are apart, one from another, but to have faith in your unity, that knows no separation.

Because the measurements of the World are not the measure of the Heart.

Objects in mirror are closer than they appear.

Carrie and Brad

There's an expression called "Fair-weather Friend". We all know the type. They may enjoy your company or be there for you ... if it's not too inconvenient, or it doesn't make them uncomfortable.

Today, the rough equivalent is "Facebook Friend". One author calls this "ambient intimacy", where you have the appearance of close relationships, but without the responsibility.

I've married couples who met online, so don't get me wrong. This isn't about the tools of the times. It's an awareness of what it all really means.

Some of us aren't fooled. Why? Because we've been through a storm or two, and know who is there for us, not just in fair weather. And hopefully we choose to be such a person for others.

And so my hope for the couple is that they recognize that which lasts through thick and thin, and let it shine as a light onto the world, an example of what real Love aspires to do – to be present without the need for convenience, or comfort, or to be entertained by constant excitement. Those are all distractions from the Real, and the Real is what I ask you to cherish today, and always.

Tara & Derek

Many people talk about 'living life to the fullest', but what does this mean? To each of us the particulars are different – different goals, different priorities, different values, a different bucket list.

But how do you live in a way you can say you're living it to the fullest? Is it something you do in between his night job, her day job, and the kids' schedules?

I say living isn't mostly about the lofty things – but those things dear and near at hand. It isn't a list of achievements or dots on a map. It is your EXPERIENCE of the journey, even those parts, or maybe especially those parts, that take you no farther than your own doorstep.

It's about the mindfulness in between planned goals – being open to the opportunities of everyday life, no matter how small. And sometimes the smallest things are the best.

So my wish for the couple is to make your lists mindfully, planning those things you share, and supporting each other in those things you don't.

Build memories as much as dreams, and always take time to find yourselves where life really is – in between, in the here and now, together.

Don't just go on your journey. BE each other's journey, for as long as you both shall live.

Kim & Chris

Sometimes it seems like extraordinary circumstances bring – or re-bring – two people together. There are words for such things: fate; coincidence; karma; destiny.

We may believe or not believe in such, but beyond all conceptions, we come here and now to the result, the reality. An amazing number of events and circumstances needed to come together to bring us where we are today, both choices and things outside our control. This eternal struggle between will and letting go is a blessing and a lesson to us all.

My wish for the couple is that whatever and however the story of their lives together is told, they can be faithful, in true mindfulness, to love in the continuing moments of their lives, every here and now, wherever and whenever they are.

Victoria & Stephen

If I say "Life is a Journey", a lot of people will probably roll their eyes at the cliché. But even for those of us who spend most of our life in the same place know that it's never really the same from day to day. There's always something different, and if we have our eyes and hearts open, life will take us to a different place each day.

When we travel, we take pictures with the unconscious hope we will bring something tangible back with us. And yet it is the memory behind the picture that gives it its value.

Studies show that people who take more pictures remember less because their brain is using the camera to outsource our memories.

But it doesn't have to be that way. A picture is worth a thousand words – if we are mindful of the feelings attached to that moment. Without that meaning – without each other, a picture is just a thousand pixels, soon buried in the Facebook wall of life.

So my wish – my blessing for you – is that every time you capture a moment, and look back, let it be a sacred act. May you always see past the image to the memory, the reality of what you've shared, that no one can delete or misplace.

Elizabeth & Richard

It's hot. People are standing. I will be brief.
Perhaps the angels and those looking down upon us might be jealous. But not because of these best of times. We assume they are in the presence of a Greater Light ... Joy ... and Peace.

No, it is because of our strivings and failings, even the injustices we've placed upon each other and must reconcile. It is in the trials of everyday life, no matter how noisy and harsh or silent and dim. It is THESE things that compel us to cling to each other, need each other, and find comfort.

In our imaginings of heaven there is always song ... and always Light. How much greater for us then to sing deliberately, and play our own role in Creation by being a Light for each other.

If there is one lesson anyone here can learn today, let it be that there is only such joy because there has been sorrow, Peace from strife, and in this imperfect world, it is not a given, but a CHOICE to Love.

Melody & Phil

Not everyone has a plan, but everyone has a story and a final destination. Some are sure of their steps and believe they know the exact path they will take. Others have no conscious compass, yet with faith and trust, move forward, step by step. By faith, we all find our way home; by faithfulness to each other, we make that home together.

Whether your map is visible to you or not, there are so many things in life both expected and unexpected. There are battles and wounds, victories and healing, hurt and forgiveness.

It is not the path, really, but what we make of the path we are given, and steps that we take, that determines what kind of home it will all lead to.

My wish for our couple here today is that they not worry about where exactly life will take them, but be ever mindful of the steps they take

No matter how you may stumble, support each other, catch each other, and ever work toward a home of happiness for you and your children. They, in turn, will learn by watching your own steps, until they find their own way to their own home someday.

Kali & Brandon

We have a glimpse of what Love is from our reading {1 Cor. 13: 1-13}, and in our hearts we know it well.

But what is "romantic"? Holding hands, eyes locking for more than a glance, candlelight, fireworks? Barry White? These are examples of things we ASSOCIATE with romance, but we can't quite put our finger on it.

It is thoughtfulness? Attention? Still not quite it.

I suggest maybe that it is being in the same time and place. I don't mean next to each other at a restaurant or just spending time together. I mean experiencing life from the EXACT same perspective, as if you were sitting in the same chair and wearing the same watch. And for a little bit, the world fades away and time stands still.

It means that they are just as much in the other's heart as they are in their own. It becomes, even for a moment, the same heart, a single heart-beat. These moments are the fulfillment of the searcher and their find, the journeyer and their destination, otherwise in some way always unreachable, untouchable, unknowable.

What did the couple first see in each other? You may never know. Because even if you were there, you weren't REALLY there, in that place.

And they were on their own time, whether they consciously knew it or not.

My wish for Brandon and Kali is that they cherish that which the world cannot see – that sacred space within their hearts – that ultimately is the same place. May you share it forever often, whenever and wherever you can.

Sylvana & Christina

Life doesn't always end up as we plan it or picture it, for ourselves or the ones we love. But I have found that if we let go, the most wondrous, unexpected things can happen.

We can try to force the universe to conform or make stories about how it should be and shake our fist at God when it isn't.

Or we can find the open door, or open our minds to the world's rules we can or even should break. We free ourselves to see beauty otherwise overlooked, to discover joy where we never thought to look, to surprise others and ourselves, to live together in peace without the need for labels, and Love without bounds.

I didn't expect my daughter's wedding to be this way. But to be honest, I didn't expect anything, because I wanted that freedom for her and myself for life to gift us with whatever should be.

And now, I could not be more proud.

Life can be sloppy, and imperfect in every way. But if I had a wish, it would be that my daughter and daughter-in-law will make it meaningful, and beautiful in every way. But I don't need to wish it, because I know that whatever happens, it will be just that.

Jessica & Patrick

Sometimes we surprise ourselves. Or do we? When we work toward a goal, it should be of no surprise that we made it — unless we had doubts. And if we have doubts and succeed, we must wonder if we did it all ourselves.

When are we truly saved? When we climb to the top of a mountain with an extra hand or water bottle? Or is it when we really don't expect to make it – or even lose hope?

Doubt is a strange thing. It can be our enemy or our ally. It can stop us from trying or even dreaming, or it can make us let go and let other forces at play move us forward, even when we can't see how it will all end.

In this respect, doubt is not only a blessing but a requirement of Faith. Only when we don't believe and are proven wrong can we see that our lives are not our own.

They belong to God. They belong to each other.

Relationships that surprise us, even when others may see it, reveal that where choice and decision and intention may falter, what is meant to be can shine through as something more – something better – than simply what we chose, decided, or even wished.

And my wish for the couple is that their whole life journey continues to be ... unexpected. Be free to doubt; be free to NOT know what the future holds. And enjoy the blessings of such a faith and faithfulness in God and each other.

Rachel & Rob

When people ask me if I could see myself married to anyone else, I think ... sure, there are a few girlfriends that might have made great partners for life. Others ... not so much.

But this isn't a compatibility equation to be worked out, the results compared, analyzed, the results published for peer review. It's not a competition, a dating game with a scoreboard and a referee that makes sure the right person wins and everyone else goes home. There's no imaginary line between fail and pass.

Some people believe in fate and providence, others choice, and free will. I'm not convinced they aren't different sides to the same coin. There are things out of our control, and things we choose, and sometimes it's a little of both. Sometimes everything lines up and you just have to say "yes" and other times you have to chisel the edges of the square to make it fit the round hole.

My words for the couple are this: Whatever you believe, wherever you find yourself, whatever you choose, it all comes together in this moment. When others dwell on what life could have been, I want you to cherish your life as it is because it ISN'T anything else. It's yours.

Dilip & Gina

There are so many words written about this sort of love. {The readings were "Union" by Robert Fulghum and a letter of Samuel Clemens to Olivia Langdon, both in the appendix on Readings}

But it is difficult to translate things of the heart. Every language, every culture has its words and concepts. Such words can mean different things at different times. They are slippery things translated into other slippery things.

This is because things of the heart have a language all to themselves. They cannot be spoken, only understood. They cannot be argued over, only shared.

Whatever words we choose are like messengers between lovers. The messenger is neither the lover nor the beloved. But when there is a true union of souls, there is no need for words. No need for a messenger, for the rest of the world is an illusion, as if in a mirror ... but to each other, you stand face to face.

Sarah & Michael

Now I myself have a wish for Michael and Sarah.

Destiny for most implies a lack of choice, of free will. {The reading preceding this was about destiny.} This is not what I believe. I believe the universe lays out a Divine Plan that takes into account the choices we will make. We are part of the process of destiny.

So what I wish for our couple is Faith. What I mean is that in the real world we do make choices and sometimes bad things – or what we decide are bad things – happen. But we still have a belief that in spite of hardships, we follow along a path of Hope, and that in the end things will be as they should.

We live our faith in such a Blessed destination by choosing to walk faithfully – together – in life.

Michael and Sarah, you have your whole lives ahead of you. Be open to the changes of who you will become, growing because of each other, and growing old but never apart. Honesty is the cure for expected misunderstandings — make it your daily bread so that you will never feel empty and find fullness in each other.

Your destiny awaits you. May you share a faith in it, across times of steadfastness and forgiveness, being faithful in every step of your journey, whatever it may bring.

Jacky & Krystle

What do you give someone who has everything? That's a challenge when you know someone who seems successful or whole or content as a person, right?

Well, how does God Bless two people's already fullness of Love?

Couples are often blessed with children and become a family. And some families are created by the union of a couple.

Just when you seem to have it all come together, the blessings are more than the sum of their parts.

But there's one other Blessing that makes the rest possible to enjoy — time.

As we get older, time seems to be something more and more finite — or even fleeting. But in truth, each moment has the potential to be stamped into a memory. And like stones in a solid foundation, these times, these memories become an ever-growing home in our hearts.

My wish for the couple is to never let ANY of the time you spend – however uneventful or ordinary it may seem – go unappreciated.

May your home for each other grow with each day, each challenge, each lazy afternoon and vacation trip, each meal, and each milestone in your children's lives.

May your family be blessed not only with time, but with an appreciation for every blessing that you truly are and become to one another.

Alexander & Jamie

The largest Cathedral is mostly made up of simple stones. Each one by itself is unimpressive. Each position they are placed in is unremarkable. It is only when one is placed upon another, deliberately, that over much time, its wondrous form takes shape.

In nature, the grandest tree is made up of simple cells. They grow themselves toward water, light, and air. It is a response to the weather and other conditions of days and seasons and years.

Deliberate or not, our lives are shaped by countless moments. Every one isn't going to be a wedding, a vacation, the birth of a child. A meal, a movie, a word, or gesture, or even silence pushes life forward most of the time.

But these things usually go unnoticed. We may seek adventure in the moment, and feel disappointed in the tedium of everyday life. And by this we miss the forest for the trees, the cathedral rising before us as we worry about the weight of a single stone.

My wish, my hope for our couple, is that you see the big picture – the adventure of life in all its moments, no matter how small or seemingly unimportant. Deliberate or not, see the adventure in EVERY moment.

Brian & Jesica

We have beliefs we hold dear, things we want to believe, things that make us a better person by believing. We can find truth in a story, a feeling, a dream, and it doesn't have to prove itself to anyone but us. This is the world of subjective truth – it is real to us personally, and we are a part of it.

At the other end, we have cold, hard facts. These are the things that don't care if you believe in them. They are still there when you turn away, or wake up. This is the world of objective truth. It is the common reality behind what we all see, even if we see it differently from where we are.

I've met a lot of couples, but the Love I see in Brian and Jesica is a truth that stretches from one end to the other. Their truth doesn't need to be seen. It is greater than what other people choose to believe. Over the course of their journey together, they have found that their truth doesn't need to be proven to anyone, or justified, or even defended. It is beyond the limits of observation, yet intimately personal at the same time.

My wish upon them is that they always have this truth, this Love, that is stronger and more real than the trials of the world around them.

Kelly & George

There's an expression that "Life finds a way". This is a scientific fact. The nature and survival of any species or system is to explore every possible way it interacts with its environment so that as times and places change, life will continue. That is why organisms exist in unimaginable places, from boiling pools to frozen ice caps, even where there is no light, or air, or soil.

But I'm not here to preach about Science.

There is also the expression "Love finds a way". This is a spiritual fact. Love surpasses all the forces of the universe in its ability to create, accommodate, heal, and fulfill. Kelly and George know this.

My wish upon them is that they never forget this spiritual fact, and harness Love as the binding force in their lives together always.

Kate & Christopher

Some people say that life begins at conception or birth, or metaphorically at this or that age. But it all depends on what you mean. There's an age when we start living for ourselves, not just a child within a family, or a student of a school. We define who we are by our choices rather than circumstance.

Some people never reach this stage.

But then some go one step farther. They choose NOT to live ONLY for themselves. They live for a greater cause. Often it is for another person, or people. They live for their spouse, their family, and their children.

So when does life really begin?

Where do you want the story to start? Does it start with your first memories of home? Does it start when you leave and make a life for yourself? Or does it start when find someone to lose yourself in, making you more than you can be, and more alive than ever?

My hope for the couple is that they find in each other the start of their story — when they truly begin to live. Adulthood may seem like entering the "real world". But when you don't go it alone, the world fades away, and Love remains — that which is REALLY real is more real than ever.

Chelsey & Mike

And now I'd like to add a few brief words. Trust is the opposite of fear, and being genuine is the hearth fire of trust. It creates a warm space to be freely oneself, freely accepting another, and gives a home to happiness.

My wish for the couple is for them to see that home is where you share this space, this freedom from fear, judgment, jealousy, resentment. May you ever tend the fire of being genuine to each other and rekindle trust any time it may dampen from the imperfections of ourselves and this world. Love, trust, be honest and happy.

Elizabeth & Michael

We go through life, and life ... is BIG. From the start, it's an endless litany of people you meet, places you go, things you do.

But it's a rare thing to find a lasting, common thread. It might be a lifelong hobby, or career, or place you can always visit or call home.

But best of all is to find someone to weave the tapestry of your life with you, however long you are blessed to have them, sometimes limited only by the span of human life itself. And whatever time we are given, we are grateful.

When you find such a person, they are no longer just another person in the story of your life, but they become a part of you, and everything else is the story. Everyone else is on the outside, and however cherished, no longer defines who you are like the one you Love. You brace yourselves as one against the World and all its challenges, its sufferings, its efforts to keep each of us lost, alone in the maze of life.

I say to you here today that Elizabeth and Mike have found trust in each other, a reflection of that trust we have in the Lord. They have surrounded themselves with each other, and found a steady ground upon which to build their home, and with hope and blessings, a family.

Ronella & Remone

Gravity. It's something we take for granted. We know that objects fall to the earth and are pulled toward each other even over great distances. The pull of our Sun on our Earth keeps us within its reach, in light, warmth, and life.

Love is the gravity of the soul. Even when we are apart, if our hearts are drawn toward one another, they will be kept in the light and warmth of each other.

For those who suffered being apart in the past, we should look to it not just as a promise or hope for a future together, but an affirmation that what can be seen as separate are in fact connected, in each other's orbits.

You know real Love for the connection that is just as strong at a distance than when together.

We can see gravity and take it for granted. My wish for this couple is that they never take for granted what cannot be seen, but is far more important.

Samantha & Justin

I tried to tie in our couple's love of fishing into a sermon. Not sure what advice makes sense here.

There are plenty of fish in the sea. Ever hear that? What they don't tell you is that it's a really big sea, and most of the fish you have to throw back.

Then there's "You teach a man to fish and you feed him for life" ... Okay, not sure that's useful either.

How about "You find someone to fish with, and your heart will never go hungry." Let's go with that.

Our lives were made for searching -- we travel the world looking for this and that. We could say we're all searching for God – a "Divine Other" – and we are truly blessed when we find God through other people. Through another human being, we can know ultimate Truth in some small, but significant, even intimate way. It's not like looking in a mirror — it's seeing face to face.

But we still have the instinct to search. In that case, once we found our fish – I mean spouse – we don't stop searching for meaning in life, we just search TOGETHER.

My wish is for this couple to never stop searching. Never stop discovering life together and through each other. May your hearts never be empty, and may all your fishing trips lead back home.

But there's one more thing. Searching has to begin somewhere, and for our couple, it began with the inspiration of the Love and commitment of relatives whose examples they wish to follow.

And so we bow our heads in a moment of silence for those who are unable to be here due to distance or time, remembering all who have gone before us and all who are here in spirit.

{Moment}

Tammy & Bruce

Now, first, if anyone thinks this outfit is strange for a wedding, you should see me at funerals. {I was dressed as the Grim Reaper at the request of the couple for their costumed theme.} Secondly, it may seem odd to talk about mortality at a wedding. But it is our limited time on this earth that motivates us to find and make meaning in our lives.

When you look at a gravestone, really look and think about it, you begin to realize what's really important in the lifetime we are given. The birth and death dates on the stone don't really matter — it's that tiny dash in between where everything happens.

Not everything brings you happiness, but everything is important, no matter how small, or painful. In being hurt, we learn how we want to be treated and how to treat others. We have to go through life's lessons, and at some point, we know the time is right to come together and form the family we are meant to have.

Most relationships won't define who we are, but they can bring us closer to those special ones that, in the end, make that tiny dash bearable, meaningful, and even joyful.

My wish for the couple? Whatever life brings, know and trust that you can make the best of it, together. May your home always be a place of refuge from the world, and all your years be filled with Love and meaning, transcending even death itself.

Melanie & Brian

People reunite from far and wide for special life events. Some are joyous, and some bring sadness. But they all present to us the opportunity to express our Love for one another in a meaningful, concrete way.

Even in darkest tragedy, new doors open. The past in not forgotten, but becomes a stepping stone to who we are. Sometimes it allows us to live a new life, not replacing one love for another, but growing into a larger, renewed family where all is cherished in the past, appreciated for the present, and ever the more hopeful for the future.

If I have one hope of my own, one blessing for this family, it is that we see all the loved ones in our lives, past, present, and future, as beloved guests in our journey, one that ends in us ALL reuniting with Him who sets us on the path. That is our hope; that is our faith; that is our Truth and Light.

Carly and Patrick

There are so many things that separate us as human beings—differences of culture, religion, politics, our favorite sports team, or what we think of pineapple on pizza.

And because those things can separate us, we are often afraid to share ourselves, to expose something that might stop someone from loving us. We are afraid what someone might think if they only knew what we've done, or what we've been through.

But for those of us who choose to Love, who prefer truth to the burden of secrets, the opposite is true. Perhaps the greatest courage is that of the heart — to allow ourselves to be vulnerable. Being sincerely who we are is an unmistakable act of trust.

This trust, this unconditional Love that we find in Carly and Patrick, teaches us that it's okay to be just as we are in all our perfection and imperfection. My hope for our couple is that they shine this sincerity, this courage of heart, into all those they Love and the world around them that desperately needs it.

Keith & Renaye

There is a certain respect or even kinship that people have for each other that comes from shared experiences. There is a certain bond between veterans, or people in a fraternity, or a profession, or survivors of physical and other traumas.

But sometimes it's not about the shared experience. Sometimes you meet someone that may be very different, but like you, had to show resolve against hard times in their life. That sort of common ground isn't backward-looking, but forward-looking.

The things we went through give us not just strength, but sometimes a compassion and understanding that another person may need. We can help those we love, not just wishing them well, but finding peace with themselves — and each other.

Sometimes, it is those things we didn't wish on ourselves that give us a connection, and someone else can see and heal, and truly accept those parts of us where otherwise we could not.

I can't wish away the past, but I can wish for Renaye and Keith to build a home upon the strength they've used to overcome their own challenges over the years.

May you find the lasting peace you are ready to share, and in turn be a light onto others.

Kerry and Bill

Sometimes it's hard to be happy.

When things go our way, we might think it's prideful to embrace joy and contentment. Sometimes we even feel guilt over whether or not we deserve it.

Or we are waiting for the other shoe to drop. We have heard too many times the phrase, "it's too good to be true". I don't think this is the ideal way to live.

A wise teacher once said to me that in the right relationship, you don't have to work at it. We might question if that makes sense, but I think I know what he was going for. It doesn't mean there won't be challenges, or effort isn't required. It means that the relationship is a source of strength rather than a draw on it.

Maybe it's the difference between trying to do something and actually doing it. We try so hard to make some relationships work while others just do. We might be wary of "Love at First Sight", quick courtships, and short engagements, but these DO often mean a lifetime of happiness, whether we deserve it or not.

My blessing is this:

Embrace whatever joy you find, and however you shall find it. Don't fear it. Don't apologize for it. Don't worry about tomorrow more than you have to. And share this gift as a family and example to all.

Ron & Joan (50th Anniversary Renewal)

A marriage is not a wedding. A wedding is a hope, a promise, a dream. A marriage is the fulfillment of all that, and more.

Times change, people change, and only over the years does that which is constant become apparent. Love proves itself. It is tested in fire.

It is simple to say "you mean everything to me". But those are only words until you live it. Those who have been through good times and bad, sickness and health, times of scarcity and abundance — those are the people who aren't just looking in a mirror of possible futures and with little time invested toward a confidence in each other. Those are the people who truly see face-to-face, in ways newlyweds cannot understand.

To the rest of the world, they may not seem like the same faces in their wedding portraits. But to each other, the people they were and have become are recognized deep inside, a vision of each other that transcends any photograph or fleeting memory.

My wishes for you: May your quarrels be fair. May you find in every frustration a cause to laugh.

The days of stalking that woman who embodied all you ever wanted are long since passed. But, may you never stop chasing her.

A wedding day full of tears is a memory. May any tears of sadness always be outweighed by those of joy.

And may you never let go of each other, with the confidence of years ever stretching toward a timeless, eternal love.

ABOUT REVEREND KEN

Ken's family faith tradition is Roman Catholic, but he embraces many religious traditions. Nicknamed "Father Ken", he served in various ministries and as a trained Catechist, certified in the Protecting God's Children® program. He later saw the need for ministering to the unchurched or those of mixed traditions. With a lifelong interest in comparative world religions, scriptural exegesis, and experience in various ministries, he decided to become an Interfaith minister credentialed through Universal Life Church and World Christianship Ministries.

Ken works under the name "Other Flock Ministries", a reference to the Gospel of John (10:16). He sees the Good News as breaking the distinction between the churched and unchurched, believers and unbelievers. To him, even theism and atheism are different perspectives that point to the same ineffable truth.

He has performed dozens of weddings, as well as funerals, last rites, and memorial services, each according to the desired traditions of those involved. As a registered hospital Chaplain, he often visits members of organizations he belongs to, such as Freemasonry.

Between serving on various boards of community organizations, he owns a web development company, but is transitioning to writing and publishing as Amorphous Publishing Guild. He is the author of "50 Shades of Pray" and "Everyday Justice". Another book is currently in the works, "Knightly Stewardship".

For more information on Ken, visit
Kenville.Net

For more information on his ministry, visit
OtherFlock.Org

OTHER WORKS BY THE AUTHOR

The books on the following pages are available worldwide. For more information, visit
Amorphous Publishing Guild

www.Amorphous.Press

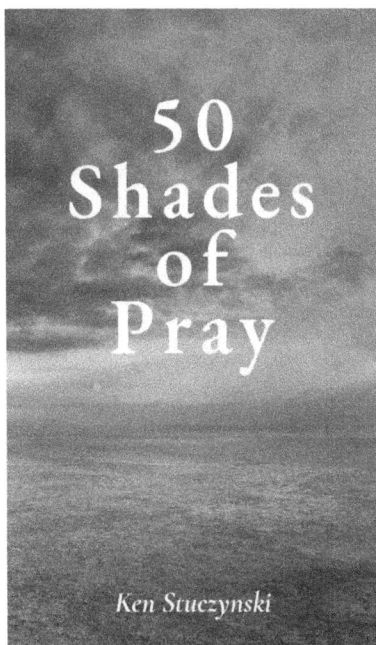

50
Shades
of
Pray

Ken Stuczynski

An easy-to-read pocket guide to
nearly fifty kinds or "shades" of
prayer. Covers opportunities
afforded by everyday life, including
emotions such as anger, and times
you just don't feel like praying. It
helps the reader reframe
prayerfulness as sharing time and
space with G–d. Suitable for people
of all faiths.

Everyday Justice

Setting the World Right
One Shopping Cart
at a Time

Ken Stuczynski

In an unjust world that seems bigger than any of us, it's easy to curse and blame. Yet we can take actions to set wrongs right, and make the world and the lives of others a little brighter. This book explores the home, the road, the marketplace, and even the future, for ways to claim our power to not be helpless and hopeless.

www.ingramcontent.com/pod-product-compliance
Lightning Source LLC
Chambersburg PA
CBHW060237030426
42335CB00014B/1506